QUANTUM AFFIRMATIONS

The New Energy Science of Conscious Manifestation

MONTE FARBER

WEISERBOOK
San Francisco, CA / Newburyport, M.

D0121661

First published in 2012 by
Red Wheel/Weiser, LLC
665 Third Street, Suite 400
San Francisco, CA 94107
www.redwheelweiser.com

Quantum Affirmations
The New Energy Science of Conscious Manifestation

For information, address:
   The Enchanted World of Amy Zerner & Monte Farber
   Post Office Box 2299, East Hampton, NY 11937 USA
   E-mail: info@TheEnchantedWorld.com
   Website: www.TheEnchantedWorld.com

For information about custom editions, special sales, premium and corporate purchases, please contact:
   Red Wheel/Weiser, LLC at 978.465.0504 or info@redwheelweiser.com

Library of Congress Cataloging-in-Publication Data available on request.

ISBN: 978-1-57863-514-6

"Universe" cover art by Amy Zerner and Jessie Spicer Zerner
Front Cover design by Dan V. Romer
Interior design by Rose Sheifer-Wright

Printed in China through Colorcraft Ltd, Hong Kong

10 9 8 7 6 5 4 3 2 1

For entertainment purposes only.

"See It, Say It, Feel It—
Live It!"

"Monte Farber is a very special soul on this planet. He assists all of us in reminding us of our true spiritual nature..."

— James Van Praagh, author of *Ghosts Among Us & Talking To Heaven*

"There are lots of gifted authors out there, but few are so creative as Monte Farber... board the "enchanted world" express, and fasten your seat belts. You're in for a wonderful ride!"

— Richard N. Bolles, author of *What Color Is Your Parachute?*

CONTENTS

*If you think you can do a thing
or think you can't do a thing,
you're right.*

—Henry Ford (1863–1947)

INTRODUCTION

As industrialist Henry Ford pointed out, if you think you are capable of doing something, the odds are that you will try as hard as you can, you won't give up easily, and eventually you will do it. If you think you cannot do something, however, it's almost certain that you won't be able to do it. In both cases, what you believe without question to be true about your capabilities, how the world works, and what you can do about it guides virtually all of your actions and, equally important, your inaction.

What we believe, however, does not have to remain etched in the stone of a mind that is hardened to change. Our beliefs can and should evolve according to our experiences, of course, but also with a good deal of our conscious direction, allowing us to move through life like a car on one of Mr. Ford's assembly lines, adding to our core beliefs what we learn from experience after experience, keeping in mind the goal of arriving at the end of the conveyor belt of life a unique (unlike Mr. Ford's cars), complete, powerful, and happy person.

Of course, this rarely happens, at least for most of us. The most successful people have a core belief system that works for them. They know they are going to succeed and they try and try again and keep on trying until they do, never taking no for an answer from anyone, including themselves.

Those without such self-confidence and a strong belief system wonder how people who do not seem any smarter than they are accumulate all that wealth and power. They marvel at how this or that unattractive person is beloved by or at least dating someone so beautiful. They eternally wonder why some people succeed and some, namely, them, fail. This book not only answers those questions; it can show you how to regain control and develop your core beliefs in a logical, fun, and scientifically based way that I evolved in response to my difficult early life. I call my technique *Quantum Affirmations* (for reasons that I explain in Chapter 2).

Let's start by defining what an affirmation actually is, or, to put it more precisely, who an affirmation is: You are an affirmation. You are what you affirm. We've already discussed how your core beliefs affect your ability to get the job done and interact with the world, but that is only the beginning. You are not just a unique and miraculously conscious collection of atoms, molecules, cells, and tissues of flesh and bone. You are you and not me or anyone else because you define yourself and differentiate yourself with the precise mix of what you affirm.

And what exactly do you affirm to be true? Do you believe in God or the Goddess? Do you believe you can get what you want in life and still be kind or do you think you have to trust no one and be ruthless? Do you think there is ultimate truth or do you think everything is a lie? Do you accept boundaries on what constitutes proper behavior or do you think everything is permitted? You define yourself to the world and even to yourself by what you believe to be true about everything under the Sun and the Moon. You are an affirmation, and what you believe is an affirmation, too.

What do you affirm to be true about yourself? I'm not talking about what you tell other people; I'm talking about what you believe in your heart and soul. You can find out what that is by taking a dispassionate listen to a small sample of the thousands of thoughts coursing through your consciousness every waking second. I'm not talking about your inspired moments, your triumphs, your loving feelings for those you care about (when they're living up to your expectations); I'm talking about the general tone of your personal thought parade.

As the Greek philosopher Socrates said, "The unexamined life is not worth living." It is well worth it to become aware of your most persistent beliefs and the tone of your thoughts about who you are, how people feel about you, how life is treating you, and all of the other things that you affirm to be true about you, other people, and the outer world. If a brief toe-dip into your stream of consciousness reveals that you're really not that self-confident or happy about yourself and where your life is now and, more to the point of this book, where your life is apparently headed, take heart. You're reading the right book.

This is a book about affirmations—my kind of affirmations: Quantum Affirmations. We've learned that you are an affirmation because of what you are affirming with your inner thoughts every minute you're awake, but the kind of affirmation this book is about is the kind that's been developed over the years as a kind of antidote to the self-defeating, paralyzing affirmations most of us have coursing through our brains. Negative affirmations are thoughts we have running through our heads like, "I can't do that because…" and "That can't happen because…," as if we, who can't do that because of…whatever, are somehow able to know beyond doubt that this or that can't happen because of…whatever. We are certain that we are uncertain, positive that we are negative about ourselves. How did things get like that inside our heads?

Life can be great, but life is often harsh. Even with the most well-meaning of parents, most of us don't get the kind of nurturing support that we need throughout our lives but that is most crucial for us to receive when we are children. All too many of us have absorbed the critical voices we heard in the past trying to manipulate us into behaving the way they thought we should. Many of the people who spoke to us that way were raised in the comparatively dark ages of the twentieth century by people who—like their own parents, who were even harsher—thought that children sometimes needed to be scolded and belittled to teach them how to behave correctly and best prepare them for dealing with the cold, cruel world.

Well, the world may indeed be cold and cruel, but it can also be wonderful. Surprisingly, it is usually both of these things at the same time, though most of us are usually so pulled by the pressures of modern life that we can see things as only either good or bad. Even more surprising is the fact that what often determines whether we see the world as good or bad is—you guessed it—what we affirm to be true. Sometimes we are like disciplined soldiers who accept without question their rank in the social hierarchy and the orders they receive from their superiors because they are certain that is how the world works; sometimes we're like frightened rabbits who are terrified that they don't know anything, even which way to run.

I firmly believe that no matter what we affirm and no matter how crazily we behave, it all makes sense to some part of our being. The fears that keep us from doing things that might benefit us but at which we might fail or for which we might be judged harshly; the behaviors that keep us isolated from relationships that might hurt us or make us feel overly dependent on others; the financial problems that keep us in the social station we are comfortable with and that are the result of our aversion to risk or our addiction to it; escapist behavior of all kinds that makes us feel safe or cut off from our fears and pain—all of our crazy affirmations make sense to some part of us that wants to keep us safe and pain-free. The trouble is that those crazy affirmations harden our lives like a plaster cast around our limbs, preventing us from walking where we want to go or reaching for the things we want and know that we should be able to have.

You cannot stop affirming things inside your mind; it's who you are, after all. You can, however, make an effort to consciously affirm what you want to be true. If you don't, it's like letting go of your car's steering wheel and expecting it to drive you where you want to go. Ah, so now you can see why things have gone the way they have!

This brings us back to the third definition of what an affirmation is. As we've discussed, first, *you* are an affirmation; second, what you believe to be true about yourself and the world is an affirmation. The third type of affirmation is shown in the kind of positive affirmations that I've written and put into a series of five affirmation decks illustrated by my incredibly beautiful—on all levels—wife and artistic collaborator, the artist and fashion designer and most positive person I know or know of, Amy Zerner.

As Amy's co-author of these five decks of affirmation training cards and several dozen books that incorporate instructions for using empowering affirmations to improve one's decision-making ability and thereby better attain one's goals, I'm always surprised to hear people express any doubt about whether affirmations can have any effect on a person's daily life.

There's no doubt that negative affirmations work (see Henry Ford's quote at the beginning of this introduction if you've forgotten why). In fact, each time I've written on the topic of affirmations I've fairly jumped out of my seat trying to get people to understand that the problem is not that they don't know how to "do" affirmations; the problem is that they're already too good at doing them—the negative ones.

Positive affirmations, like the one I call my Master Affirmation,

I have all that I need to get what I want

are designed to be said repeatedly to ourselves, either aloud or in our heads, in the hope that they will mitigate or completely counteract the negative affirmations I mentioned previously ("I can't do that because...") and "That can't happen because...") the way antacid tablets counteract acid indigestion.

The connection between what we affirm to be true and the life we experience is so strong that even the most basic affirmation techniques can and sometimes do produce measurable, positive changes in the lives of those who are sincere and regular practitioners of positive affirmations. They are the exception, however, and not the rule. This book and my Quantum Affirmations technique are designed to be like prescription-strength antacid medicine to give you the self-confidence to counteract the negative affirmations so you can attain a calm inner mind. At the risk of sounding like one of those high-pressure pitchmen on TV: But wait, there's more—a lot more.

In *Quantum Affirmations*, I share with you the method I evolved over the course of the most difficult periods of my life, a method for transforming what I affirm to be true about myself and what it is possible for me to experience. In this way, I empowered myself to profoundly transform my then sorrowful life into a daily experience of love, light, and laughter, and in *Quantum Affirmations*, I will teach you how you can change your life for the better the way I have; I will show you how to reach into the future and "plant your flag" there, claiming the future that you want like an explorer claims a new, uninhabited island.

I am not an accredited teacher or psychologist or a quantum physicist. I am, however, a living example of a self-made Renaissance man. I am someone who "followed my bliss," as the late, great Joseph Campbell so famously said. More to the point of this book, I am a successful, highly intuitive person who has devoted his life to helping other people improve their own decision-making ability and find their own version of success.

My version of success, the one I am confident I can show you how to achieve, is simply this:

I wake up every morning when I want to because I work for myself. As if the absence of alarm clocks wasn't amazing enough, there right next to me is my incredible wife and soulmate, and we've been together in love and lust for thirty-six years. We are, as of this writing, relatively fit and healthy, especially for our age. We live in a beautiful house that we laughingly say is a factory with bedrooms because we are both quite productive. Our running joke is that we didn't want to have nine-to-five jobs, so we ended up having ninety-five jobs. We have what is really a mom-and-pop mini-conglomerate whose "brand" is The Enchanted World because that is the world we want to keep living in and share with those whose world is not so enchanted at the moment. We make a comfortable living doing what we love and are proud of—making art, books, games, clothing, jewelry, DVDs, and both spoken word and music CDs—and we do everything to the best of our ability to help others and beautify the world. See? I told you I'm living a life worth living. You can have your own version of what I've attained; of that I'm sure, because I'm really good at helping people help themselves. In fact, we have helped a lot of people, and we're only just getting started, because *Quantum Affirmations* is the culmination of my life's work.

So, without further ado, now that we've been introduced to each other and to the three-dimensional meaning of the word *affirmation*, let's get on with teaching you my Quantum Affirmations technique so you can change your future. You'll find that it is surprisingly easy and fun to do, and if you stick with it for a few weeks, I think you'll find that it works as if by magic!

My Quantum Affirmations are not like typical affirmations, and this book, not so coincidentally entitled *Quantum Affirmations*, is not your typical self-help book; it is most certainly not your typical affirmations book. Those books, while well-intentioned, usually offer only the basics of using the power of positive thinking. They teach that if you simply affirm the positive statements they suggest, like "Every day in every way I get better and better," which you may or may not believe to be true, you can somehow undo the effects of your years of affirming negative statements like the two we've already discussed, "I can't do that because..." and "That will never happen because..." (which, let's face it, you definitely believe to be true). Those are only two examples of the kind of powerful, negative, self-limiting affirmations that we all have to deal with successfully if we are ever going to experience the kind of life we know in our hearts we are meant to live. That's where my Quantum Affirmations technique comes in.

An overwhelming majority of those who buy self-help books do not get enough positive results, and so they discontinue their practice and rightly conclude that those affirmations are not as powerful as advertised, certainly not powerful enough to change their life in a meaningful way.

My Quantum Affirmations are designed to produce results that are not only powerful but also fun to do; you develop your creative spirit as you create your new life.

Like me, my Quantum Affirmations techniques came into life the hard way. I evolved them in the same way that doing rough work produces calluses, as my reaction to the real and difficult challenges of my life. I think that's why after our blessed meeting in 1974, I was able to hold up my end of creating our blessed life with Amy. These formerly secret techniques—so secret that even I didn't know that I had developed them—have helped me not only to survive the dark, lonely first part of my life, but to thrive as Amy and I created and continue to create our enchanted life together. I affirm that they enabled me to realize how rare and valuable it was for me to be living with Amy and her dear mother, the late, great pen-and-ink master artist, Jessie Spicer Zerner, an experience I cherish and maintain through the psychic ability Jessie's passing forced me to discover in myself—I missed her so much and still do, even though she's in my psychic imagination always.

I know all too well that nothing lives forever in this world. All I can say is, so far, so really, really good. Amy and I have enjoyed our thirty-six years filled with love, laughter, and making a good living from and enjoying recognition for our creative gifts. Just as Cupid was the child of Mercury (communication) and Venus (beauty), our books and Amy's art, couture clothing, and jewelry are all "children" of our desire to imbue everything we create for others to buy with love, beauty, and practical wisdom to improve their life in some way.

I bless the day I decided to write *Quantum Affirmations* because it was only then, when I sat down to see if I could figure out exactly how I had created my half of our wonderful life, that I became aware of the techniques I had developed organically, to the point where they were second nature and, like water to a fish, invisible to me. Until then, I hadn't realized that I was approaching life quite differently from the majority of people in our world today, who are living Henry David Thoreau's often quoted line:

> *The mass of men lead lives of quiet desperation.*

Amy and I have, instead, led lives of high quality and profound meaning. The best way for me to say thank you to the universe for my good fortune is to share my Quantum Affirmations techniques with you and help you to attain your goals, if not right now, then in the very near future. In fact, *Quantum Affirmations* is all about changing your future from where you're headed without my techniques to the much better place you can get to by using them.

Writing is like journeying into the future while both driving where you want to go and looking out the window daydreaming. We have now come to the first take-away for you from my Quantum Affirmations process:

> Sharing your blessings is a powerful way to ensure that they continue to flow to and through you.

Like everything else in this book, it may sound like wishful thinking, like it may be too easy to actually produce powerful, measurable results. All I ask is that you try it and see if it works for you like it works for me and Amy and the five real people you are going to meet as they learn how to do their version of my Quantum Affirmations. (Hint: It does!)

Thank you for giving me a chance to prove to you that I can teach you how to manifest in your life the same kind of love, success, and contentment that I've co-created with my brilliant wife, whose wisdom and faith in me allowed me to rediscover the landscape of my soul and map it for your benefit. I am confident that if you put into practice what I am about to teach you, it's going to seem that your luck has changed. You and I, however, will know that luck had very little to do with it.

CHAPTER 1

WHAT DOES QUANTUM MEAN?

Most people have heard the word *quantum*, especially as it's used in the term *quantum leap*, which is often used to indicate a sudden and significant change, especially one that involves an increase of power or understanding.

Doing my Quantum Affirmations has significantly changed and empowered my life and the lives of the people you will meet within the pages of this book. Understanding and performing your own version of my Quantum Affirmations can change your life, too, but how much your life can change is totally up to you. In fact, the very word *quantum* comes from the Latin word *quantus*, meaning "how much" or "how great." So how much do you want to change your life? That much? Okay, I believe that you can make a quantum leap—and my Quantum Affirmations can help. How great is that?!

Please forgive my having fun with the previous wordplay. I know you are reading this book because things are difficult for you right now and you want to improve your life, not admire my sense of humor. I believe, however, that keeping your sense of humor burning inside you is an important part of learning any technique, especially one whose goal is self-improvement. It was my sense of humor that got me through my sad early years, and it keeps me going every day in the face of life's challenges. When I have a bad day it is almost always because I've lost my sense of humor and have taken some annoyance or even a series of them way too seriously.

I have never been interested in any spiritual practice, belief system, or ceremony where you couldn't laugh or otherwise express joy. You can imagine my delight when I met and studied with one of the twentieth century's great philosophers, Professor Arnold Keyserling of the University of Vienna, who told us unequivocally, "If you can't laugh, it's not sacred." Having one of your core beliefs confirmed by someone you respect is a sign that you are on the right path. This happened to me again when I read this opening line of one of the Dalai Lama's books, "The purpose of life is to be happy," and I thought, *That's what I've always thought!* Laughter really is the best medicine in the Native American sense of medicine, which Professor Keyserling told us is "that which makes you whole."

So even though we all have a long list of improvements we'd like to see in our experience of life—more love and money, less pain and sorrow, to name just a few—it is important that we keep our sense of humor as we go about improving our lot. We also have to appreciate what we have, because if you don't appreciate what you have, you won't appreciate what you get. My Quantum Affirmations are going to help you get what you want, but they won't work if you don't appreciate what you already have. To be grateful for what you have puts you in the perfect frame of mind for best using my Quantum Affirmations techniques.

> *Gratitude is not only the greatest of virtues,*
> *but the parent of all the others.*
> —Marcus Tullius Cicero (106—43 BCE)

We've all made choices that have guided us on our path to where we are today, for good or ill. When you realize how lucky you are to be alive and able to read and think and even attempt to do something to improve your situation, it becomes clear that the best thing you can do about your mistakes and problems and challenges is to laugh at them, be grateful for where you are today, and do all you can to improve your situation. Laughter also puts you in the zone of creativity, a mental state of relaxed concentration, where learning can take place.

You've already thought about how much you want to change your life, but there's one more thing you have to ask yourself: How much do you love yourself? There is a kind of cultural prohibition against loving oneself for fear of becoming one of those sorry people who seem to love themselves at everyone else's expense: serial adulterers, narcissists, egomaniacs, politicians, and similarly self-involved people. I do not mean to suggest that you love yourself to the exclusion of everyone else. I'm talking about what for most of us is simply liking yourself—stopping for a moment the incessant self-criticism and negativity about what you have or haven't done and forgiving yourself, the way I hope you would forgive a child or a loved one who made the exact same mistake you find unforgivable when you are the one who has made it.

Albert Einstein, the genius and pioneer of quantum theory, from whom you'll hear a lot more later on in this book, defined insanity as "doing the same thing over and over again and expecting different results." If you're reading this book, you probably have a tendency to be overly critical of yourself. If you want to get the most out of my Quantum Affirmations technique, it's time to try a different approach to living and especially to motivating yourself to take action to change your life: love yourself more. Don't worry, you won't become an egomaniacal narcissist—I won't let you! (Hmm...I may have gotten more than a little grandiose myself!)

Have faith you'll keep your ego in check. Give your inner critic a rest. It's time to call back into the game of life the part of you that loves you like the little child you are, a part of you that has not been in the game for so long that you can be sure it is rested, energized, and ready for action. So, sense of humor switched on? Check! Willing to try to love yourself more? Check! Okay, you're ready. It's time to play Quantum Affirmations!

CHAPTER 2

WHAT IS A QUANTUM AFFIRMATION?

The funny thing regarding Quantum Affirmations—and here's the bad news and the good news—is that you don't have to learn how to do them at all! The reason you need to read this book and learn my way of doing Quantum Affirmations is not because you don't know how to do them; the problem is that you are too good at doing them and, in fact, you are probably doing one right now. Let me explain.

Perhaps you are thinking, "Monte's wrong. I don't know how to do Quantum Affirmations," and you're visualizing yourself not knowing how to do Quantum Affirmations and then continuing to watch the "movie" of this scenario in "your mind's eye," as Shakespeare so beautifully put it. And perhaps you saw in an instant that I don't know what I'm talking about, and you saw yourself putting down and forgetting about this book, regretting that you had bought it, despairing that once again you had bought a book trying to improve your life but it had been a failure. And if then your mind made all kinds of connections and associations with what you were thinking, causing your thoughts to spin off in all directions of negative thinking about yourself and your past and your future and me and this book, and only you know what else, congratulations! You've just done a Quantum Affirmation and proved me right.

One of the reasons your affirmation was a Quantum Affirmation was that you created this movie in your head about the whole thing and you believed it without question. I don't hold it against you. We are in the early pages of our relationship, you and I, and we're just getting to know each other. There I was claiming you knew how to do Quantum Affirmations when you had just spent your hard-earned money on the book precisely because you didn't know how to do them. You were totally convinced that you were right, and you saw every aspect of the situation, including the scenes of yourself putting this book down and maybe trying to get your money back. You created a complete movie of the past, present, and future of your buying, reading, and returning this book, and you did a great job. My Quantum Affirmations technique is designed to help you make use of your ability to create these mental movies for the purpose of telling your powerful subconscious mind what you want to be your real life in the not-too-distant future. It may sound like wishful thinking, but I believe that there is actually a scientific basis for why my techniques have worked so well for me, Amy, and the many people we've trained how to do them.

The reason I call my technique Quantum Affirmations is because although I make my living as a psychic Tarot-reading astrologer who invents games that teach these and other metaphysical subjects, I have affirmed since my youth that I am a serious, scientific, and skeptical person who doesn't believe anything until it's been proven to me beyond a reasonable doubt. I try to stay current with the goings-on in science, medicine, psychology, and every subject that helps to explain and improve the human condition and the natural world. When I analyzed the techniques I had been using and evolving throughout the course of my life to keep improving my daily experience and finally identified as being crucial to my creating my wonderful life, I noticed that these techniques bore striking similarities to some of the basic and most proven tenets of quantum mechanics, the most far-out branch of physics.

> *I believe in intuition and inspiration. Imagination is more important than knowledge. For knowledge is limited, whereas imagination embraces the entire world, stimulating progress, giving birth to evolution. It is, strictly speaking, a real factor in scientific research.*
> —Albert Einstein (1879—1955)

I am not a scientist, but if I was, I would most like to be like Albert Einstein, the man who proved that all matter is essentially energy, one of the most powerful spiritual statements possible. When I first read the above quote I felt as if he had "knighted" me, a person intuitive to the point of being demonstrably psychic, and granted me a seat at his round table of intuitive knights and even license to use the terms of quantum mechanics in an experimental way.

In the early twentieth century, scientists like Albert Einstein, Niels Bohr, Werner Heisenberg, Erwin Schrödinger, and Max Born (who coined the term *quantum mechanics*) applied their genius to the attempt to understand the workings of particles at the atomic and subatomic levels. They wanted to know the "how much" of every particle and its interactions with every other particle.

The main reason I call my technique Quantum Affirmations is because of quantum mechanics' theory of probable futures and parallel universes and especially because of my technique's similarity to the quantum mechanics concept of "entanglement."

Two atomic or subatomic particles that interact with each other in some way—perhaps they come close enough so as to be virtually touching, for example—are said to become "entangled." When two particles are entangled, that means that even if they each go on their merry way and even if they end up on opposite sides of the universe, they are still somehow in communication! Quantum physicists and mathematicians have proved that spinning or otherwise affecting one particle will affect the other entangled particle *instantly*, faster than the speed of light! Einstein called this "spooky action at a distance," but he couldn't disprove it, and it has become an accepted part of quantum mechanics.

My Quantum Affirmations technique is designed to entangle you right here and now with the probable future you want to get to—one of many possible futures your present situation and affirmations are directing you to. By entangling you in the present moment with the probable future that you want to reach, it greatly increases the probability that you will actually reach that future.

I realize that this is a lot of theories to take in at the same time. All I ask is that you bear with me and give my theory a fair hearing. While you do, please realize that the quantum mechanics theories have been proven to be true, no matter how weird they may sound. What I'm asking you to do is to keep an open mind about whether those proven laws of quantum physics are at work in the subatomic world of affirmations, which are made up of pure energy unfettered by observable form except in our mind's eye.

CHAPTER 3

QUICK GUIDE
THE FIVE KEYS OF QUANTUM AFFIRMATIONS

It may be a good idea to make a photocopy of the following quick guide so you can carry it with you while you're learning to do my Quantum Affirmations techniques. That way you won't forget anything. I'm going to expand a little on this quick guide right below it, and then I'll examine each technique in depth in its own chapter.

A Quick Guide to Monte Farber's
Quantum Affirmations Technique

1. Identify Your Goal—What do you really want?

2. Examine Your History with That Goal—Why haven't you attained it?

3. Identify Your Gift—What flows to you effortlessly and endlessly?

4. Entangle Your Gift with Your Goal—
Work your gift to attain your goal.

5. Create a "Quantumplaytion"—The miracle is in your mind.

Let me flesh out my quick guide to my Quantum Affirmations technique:

Step 1. Identify Your Goal.

What do you really want? Upon examination, you may find that you don't want exactly what you first thought you wanted. You may think you want *that* but upon close examination find that you really want THAT!

Step 2. Examine Your History with That Goal.

Why do you want what you really want? Why do you think you haven't gotten it yet?

Step 3. Identify Your Gift.

What flows to you effortlessly and endlessly? What ability do you have that you are so confident about that you have no doubt? It can be anything from the simplest human ability to the most complex. Everyone has at least one gift. Kindness is always available.

Step 4. Entangle Your Gift with Your Goal.

Here's where the entanglement happens. You visualize with certainty a scene where, when you do what flows to you endlessly and effortlessly, you also, by so doing, attain your goal. For example, if you want money or love, you see yourself doing what you are good at, and you see money or love or whatever your goal flowing out of your doing so.

Step 5. Create a "Quantumplaytion."

Create the future in what I have named your "quantumplaytion." This, of course, is a play on the word *contemplation*, a word whose meaning derives from *templum*, the same Latin word from which *temple* originates. The word *templum* meant a space marked out for the Roman official charged with observing and interpreting omens, also known as divination; in short, a place for predicting the future!

Your quantumplaytion is where the magic of my Quantum Affirmations technique happens. Applying your gift to your goal at the very least calms you down and gives you hope, whether or not you believe, as I do, that it entangles something that is easy for you to attain with something that you have been unable to attain. Your quantumplaytion seals the deal. In it, you consciously direct the production in your mind's eye of an elaborate visualization, complete with sights, sounds, and especially feelings you will experience in the future you want to attain, complete with any and all negative consequences, secure in the knowledge that you are dealing successfully with them, whatever they may be. It is crucial that your quantumplaytion be as real to you as you can make it, warts and all.

And that's it. That's all you have to do to undo your years of reciting your internal mantra-liturgy-chant of negative affirmations and create the life you've always wanted to be living. You don't even have to do your practice all the time, just when you wake up and before you go to sleep.

When you become aware of a major negative affirmation hurricane going on in your head, because you're anxious or worried or scared or have succumbed to whatever sets you off, you can do one or more of your Quantum Affirmations techniques or, if you're pressed for time, one of my thirty-six supercharged Quantum Aspirations, which you'll find in Chapter 15. After a few weeks of practice, you may be surprised to see yourself noticing what sets you off and nipping your anger or worry or fear in the bud.

As dear Professor Keyserling was told by his friend the philosopher George Gurdjieff (1866—1949), "When falling asleep wakes you up, you're making progress." Becoming more conscious of your habitual ways of thinking, acting, and reacting is another benefit of your Quantum Affirmations practice. Once you do, you are better able to avoid time-wasting mistakes and make the most beneficial decisions and course corrections in your journey through time.

Quantum physics states that there is no reason for time to only move forward, it can move backward, too! To me, this offers a scientific explanation for miracles like spontaneous healing and otherwise inexplicable appearances and disappearances. The past and the future can actually be affected in the present moment. This concept also supports the power of my Quantum Affirmations to affect your future and maybe even your past.

We've all seen movies about time travel, in which a character goes back in time to change something in the past so as to affect the future from which he or she has come. Quantum Affirmations are similar in that you are aware that what you are doing in the present can and will change your probable future. I look at it as a blending of science and magic, with science being the things that we can understand and prove through replication, and magic being the things we see happening with surprising regularity and yet we neither understand them nor can prove them except through our own experience of the changes in our lives being real and in line with our Quantum Affirmations.

I am also confident that you will soon begin to notice changes in your experience of daily life that are in line with the changes you are seeking to make to your future as a result of your Quantum Affirmations practice. These changes can be subtle or they can be sudden and indisputable. Usually, one kind of change feeds the other and so on. This is how Quantum Affirmations is designed to work.

CHAPTER 4

STEP ONE
IDENTIFY YOUR GOAL—WHAT DO YOU WANT?

> What do you really want?
> Upon examination, you may find that you don't want exactly what you first thought you wanted. You may think you want *that* but upon close examination find that you really want THAT!

Quantum Affirmations is a book about getting what you want. But what exactly do you want? Almost everyone believes they know exactly what they want. After counseling thousands of people, however, I have to say that this is most often not the case. Most people think they know what they want, but though they're often quite close, they're not as clear as they need to be to manifest the kind of life changes they truly desire.

For example, many, many women and far too few men come to me with questions about finding their soulmate. As someone who found his soulmate at the tender age of twenty-four years old and considers his real life as starting from that day, I know how valuable meeting your soulmate is. I do not believe, however, that *that* is the true desire of everyone who says that they want to find their soulmate.

What most people want is to not be lonely. *That* is what they want, and that is what they should be looking to first create in their life *before* they move on to finding their soulmate! It is quite possible for a person to live alone, not find their soulmate, and yet not feel lonely. It is also a lot more likely to happen than finding your soulmate (without using Quantum Affirmations, of course!). When it comes to figuring out what you want, it's best to get down to the basic problem you are trying to solve before you start aiming for what are actually the secondary things you want to attain. And attain them you will, especially if you plan your Quantum Affirmations program in a logical, attainable order.

Many years ago I had to get somewhere fast late at night and hailed a New York City taxi to get me there. I offered to pay the driver double the meter if he would only get me uptown in fifteen minutes. He turned around to stare at his young and desperate fare. I was staring back at a classic old-timer, complete with a fraying, oil-stained driving cap and chewed-up unlit cigar stuck in his unshaven face. Finally, he said, "I'll get you there in time, kid. All you got to do is sit back and shut up." He proceeded to drive a lot slower than I wanted him to, but this expert driver made every traffic light so we never had to stop, and we got uptown with minutes to spare. My point is that sometimes the best way to get to where you want to go is not to rush but to plan your goals in an order that is achievable. In my experience, goals are attained this way and often in a manner that can appear quite magical.

So…what do you want? We are going to ask that question until you and I are satisfied with the answer. And to give us a little more incentive to figure out what, exactly, we are going to be using as our goal for our first Quantum Affirmations experience, here is a powerful secret known to those ancient Roman officials charged with observing and interpreting omens and passed down to all expert practitioners of the divinatory arts, of which I am most certainly one:

> **If you know your question, you know your answer.**

The process of identifying precisely what you want to know usually leads you on a journey that, though fraught with many dead ends, usually leads you to a place very near your question's ultimate answer. Figuring out exactly what you want will make it much easier for you to actually get it. You will also know what you do not want, and that will keep you from wasting your valuable time.

As a psychic Tarot reader and astrologer, I am paid to do my best to help people learn if and when they are going to get what they want. If getting what they want is not in the cards, then it's my job to advise them on the best way to adjust their thoughts and their behavior in order to change their fate and link up with a probable future in which they do get what they want.

Quantum Affirmations are second only to real-world experiences as the best way to adjust your thoughts and bring them in line with the actions you must take to get what you want. In fact, our affirmation card decks and more than half of our published works are designed to help you get what you want. That makes me acutely aware of just how difficult that question can be for many people: "What do you want?"

Of course, the word *want* has two meanings. "To desire" is the one that springs to mind, but *want* also means "to lack, be without, have need of." You get the picture, figuratively and literally, for our affirmations are designed to help you get in real life what you picture in your mind. So the question is not just, What do you want? It's, What do you desire? What do you lack? What do you need? They all apply.

Not being clear about what you want, including not being clear if you really need something or just desire it, can be one of the biggest impediments to your getting what you want. Conversely, knowing what you want and whether or not you actually need it can be one of the best ways to ensure that you are going to get what you're going after. Remember, *If you know your question, you know your answer.* The process of making your questions as precise as possible also clarifies your mind and helps you to see answers before, during, and after your session with a reader like me. It's a beautiful thing.

But even when you are well into your Quantum Affirmations practice, it will always be wise to ask yourself, "What do I want now?" It's like steering a ship on the open sea; you have to keep correcting your course as you go. You think you know what you want, what you need, but as you move toward your goal, what you want and need shift, and you have to shift your goal and adjust the affirmations that will help take you where you want to go. Asking, "What do I really want? What do I really need?" and accepting what comes back to you as your answer is the way to go, no matter how odd it might seem.

When I do a psychic reading for someone, I ask that person, "What do you want to know?" because that's the way I've trained myself to flip the switch and fire up my psychic synapses. I wasn't born psychic; I worked hard to improve my intuition and to write our series of books helping others improve theirs. My psychic gift is the result of my doing all that work plus doing the work of thousands of readings for people from all walks of life, everywhere I go.

There is a basic principle of alchemy: You cannot create gold unless you first possess it. This means that you have to perfect your unexamined human life as best you can before you can move on to the seemingly magical realms of chemistry and science. Although my friends laugh when I say it, I feel that I'm a classically trained psychic because, as was the case in the ancient mystery schools, I did not allow myself to try using psychic abilities until I had first learned astrology, Tarot card reading, alchemy, and other intuition-building techniques. Then dear Jessie's passing impelled me to graduate, take off my psychic training wheels, and contact the other side, the great hall of the Akashic Records, the place from which my information comes.

I use the question "What do you want to know?" as a trigger for the psychic information to start flowing, because otherwise I wouldn't be able to be around people without information about them coming to me. The reason I mention this is so that you won't feel odd if you're not sure exactly what you want. You are in good and large company. You'd be surprised at how difficult it is for people to decide what they want to know, what they need to know, even when I'm asking them. They often say, "Can't you just read me?" and I say, truthfully, "No." I ask them to ask me what they'd ask the future or a departed loved one, and that usually gets things started on the right track.

So what do you want? What do you desire? What do you feel that you lack and need in order to get what you want? Take your time. Be honest, and even if what you want is something that other people and even you don't understand, you must accept it and be kind to yourself.

Judging and blaming is a waste of time. We're much better off filling our heads with positive affirmations to replace the negative affirmations we've been doing since we could talk, even if the positive affirmations sound so… positive! I find it hilarious how we accept the negative affirmations as "realistic," but the positive affirmations are often viewed by those new to the process as "phony," no matter how many difficult and amazing things we've accomplished.

Did you ever wonder why some people are so successful or have the things that you want? It's because they don't drag themselves down with negative affirmations. They don't just believe in themselves; they "be/live" in themselves, living and being in the world of their own version of my Quantum Affirmations, a world where what they want is, to them, as real and certain to exist as it can be. Are they a bit self-involved? Perhaps, but if you've ever wondered how people—who you know are no smarter than you—accomplish such great things and have the life you've only dreamed off, well, maybe it's time to get a bit more self-involved, no?

Many successful people do positive affirmations naturally, and so will you, once you've done it unnaturally for a time. How long? That's up to you. You'll definitely start doing them in a more heartfelt manner when you notice that you've actually attained a small goal or two, so start small with your desires. Don't try to win the lottery; try shooting for a raise or a better job. And don't think it's going to have to happen magically. You can ask for a raise after you've done positive affirmations to strip away any anxiety, defensiveness, or fear that you're not going to get it—you know how animals can sense fear, and you know your boss is an animal, so it's best to prepare yourself with positive affirmations. Do your affirmation with the goal being to give you the confidence you need to get what you want and the wisdom to know when to speak and when to keep silent. You're allowed to ask for what you want, but you need to do it at the right time. And you're allowed to be happy, as happy as you can be. So what would make you happy?

Wouldn't it make you happy if I gave you an affirmation that would work and help you get on the road to a better life? Well, if you recall, I already did give you the Master Affirmation, and I hope you noticed how good it felt when you said it that one time:

> ## I have all that I need to get what I want.

You can say it anytime. If you say it to yourself or even out loud if you're alone, and if you realize that it is true and realize that more and more as you say it more and more—especially when negative affirmations try to regain their control of the radio station playing 24/7 in your head—you can expect to see some changes for the better in your life. There are no guarantees as to how long this will take; that is totally dependent on how you feel about you, what you want, and what you need, and how dedicated you are to your affirmation practice. You get the picture, again, in your mind's eye.

Remember, Quantum Affirmations is powerful because it asks you to unleash your creativity and let it run around for a while in the backyard of your mind. You can improvise on any and all of the affirmations, exercises, and information I give you. I'm not one of those teachers who want you to do everything exactly the way I do it—quite the contrary. I want you to use my training as an introduction to your own interpretation of what you get from my training. For example, since we're trying to get to the heart of what exactly we want to set as our Quantum Affirmations goal, we can get creative with the Master Affirmation and adjust it to say

> ## I have all that I need to know what I want!

I would hope that by now you have a good idea of exactly what you want. Whatever it is, that is what you have to set as your goal for your Quantum Affirmations process. As long as it is reasonable and lawful and doesn't harm you or anyone else, you have my blessings and the blessings of your powerful subconscious mind and whatever deity or deities you are comfortable envisioning as supporting you.

If you are comfortable with and desire the blessings of a deity or deities, then please be aware that on the spiritual level, your ultimate desire should be contentment in all circumstances and nothing less. Oh, forgive me, I said the *should* word, a big New Age no-no. Well, I don't care. If you ask for the blessings, favor, and power of anyone or anything, you have to play by their rules, and "they" on the other side know that the goal of a fully realized human being is contentment in all circumstances, and so they'll help you to the best of their abilities if your goal is part of your path to that beautiful way to live. I haven't attained it yet, but that doesn't mean I'm not on my way.

If you want to find love, money, a job you love, or a new car, you can have that, too. Here is another of my secret tips for dealing with the spirits, in this case, *your* spirit. I have proven to myself beyond doubt that to be content, not only do you need to have what you want; you first need to want what you have. When you want what you have, then instantly, you have what you want! It may sound like just more of my wordplay (and it is, of course), but it also happens to be true, and it's a powerful way to prime your manifestation pump and get you on your path to your goal.

Try it, even for a few moments. Take a vacation from the feeling of lack and desire and inadequacy that all too often is the way those of us who are aware of what we want think we need to motivate ourselves. I want you to do this and feel good about yourself, even though you do not have what you thought you needed so desperately. Here's the Master Contentment Affirmation:

> I want what I have; therefore, I have what I want.

Alternate that with

> I have all that I need to get what I want.

We all have needs and wants and desires. What we don't all have, especially the most successful of our species, is feelings of inadequacy without possessing things and having things be a certain way. Come on, you know it's true. You can be happy without having lots of possessions, which end up possessing you. Contentment, not winning the lottery, is the goal. If you win the lottery without having contentment, you will still be in the same state of want as you are right now, because there is always more to want.

I have many wealthy clients, and I have known many wealthy people in my life, and not one of them thinks that they are rich, because they know someone who is much richer than they are! I always think of myself as rich, and I even say it sometimes, and it surprises people, especially those who know how much richer in terms of money and possessions they are than I am.

But when I point out to them that the things that I have that make me feel so very fortunate also make me feel rich, because what I have is a life of true wealth, they see my point and they see that, yes, I am one of the richest people they know or know of. It doesn't take money or power or fame or anything material to make a person rich. If you want what you have and have what you want...if you're relatively healthy...if you have any reason to feel content and are wise enough to concentrate on your feeling of contentment, then you are richer than almost anyone.

What do you want? What do you need? What do you lack? If you said "contentment," then you're waking up to life and on your way to being truly wealthy and to attaining every goal you set for yourself. Quantum Affirmations work best when your manifestation engine is ready to roar, unimpeded by sludge such as unreasonable expectations and self-doubt. Now that you know what you want, it's time: Gentlewomen, gentlemen, start your engines!

CHAPTER 5

STEP TWO
EXAMINE YOUR HISTORY WITH YOUR GOAL

> Why do you want what you really want?
> Why do you think you haven't gotten it yet?

Okay, gentlewomen and gentlemen, you've started your engines and they're purring along, fueled by the power you get when you finally know exactly what you want to get at this stage of your Quantum Affirmations process. Before you roar on down the racetrack to your goal, however, it might be a good idea to take a look at the road ahead. The analogy of a racetrack is a perfect one because not only is it important to know about what's in front of you—the future—but it is important to know what is happening behind you—the past—because like on a racetrack, what is now behind you will soon be coming up in front of you in the form of the future results of your past actions and attitudes.

Now that you've examined your goal and drilled down to what you would like to see in your future experience of daily life, I believe it is a good idea to reflect for a moment upon what you believe is the reason that you do not already possess it. If I had to pick one word to describe the reason why most people do not already have what it is that they want, I would have to say the word is *fear*.

In the centuries-old traditions of reading Tarot cards, there is a way of laying the cards on the table, what we Tarot readers refer to as a "spread," called the Celtic Cross. The last card laid out represents the final outcome of your reading, but it is the next-to-last position that is applicable to our examination of how fear can keep a person from having what he or she wants. This position is known as "the hope or the fear," and for many years I couldn't understand how both meanings could apply to the same card. One day it hit me. The ancient Tarot readers understood that what a person only hopes for is something that, at the time of their reading, they are not comfortable with. In essence, what they hope for but do not possess is something that they are afraid of.

I'm not saying that you are terrified of success or wealth or love or relationships or of looking your best. I am saying that when you are a little afraid or otherwise made anxious about that which you only desire but do not have, that can have the effect of preventing you from operating at your optimal level. Living in fear makes you think and act in ways that keep away from your grasp that which you desire. Even at the best of times it takes sustained and conscious effort to keep our counterproductive patterns from interfering with our drive to achieve our goals. Fear can be paralyzing—think about the fight or flight or freeze reaction in our fellow animals—and fear often makes it difficult, if not impossible, to get what we want. Fortunately, truth, forgiveness, and Quantum Affirmations can help to convince fear to stop trying so hard to protect us and go back to its ready room and wait for something that we actually should be afraid of before it jumps down the fire pole, ready to go.

I think fear is such an important issue that a good use of our time would be to examine here and now how it can affect the four areas of life I worked on with the people I counseled for this book and whom you will meet in subsequent chapters. These areas are *success, wealth, love/relationships,* and *weight loss.*

SUCCESS

The fear of success is a cliché, and with good reason; it is present in everyone, including the successful. The successful experience the fear of success the way people experience the thrill of a roller coaster or a horror movie, the way most actors experience the stage fright that is a natural part of their careers—they all love it!

Can you change your attitude toward success and start to love your natural fear of it? I hope so. I don't have any inclination to start loving roller coasters and horror movies, because I have enough ups and downs and frightening moments in my ninety-five jobs and my role as an "outsider" career performance artist. As your friend and mentor, I suggest that you embrace the fear of success as a natural and even a desirable emotion; savor it like a rare and expensive wine. You've had enough of your cheap whine—

as in "Why can't I be successful?"—haven't you? I know, more wordplay, but you know there's some method to my madness by now. And if we can't laugh at ourselves and our situations, then we may not be in the best mental and emotional state to take action to improve our lives.

WEALTH

Here's another easy one. The main reason most people are not wealthy is the obvious one: They don't take the time to learn the basics of managing their money—budgeting, saving, investing, self-denial—and they don't like rich people. Does that sound odd to you? If so, think about it in terms of what we're learning about my Quantum Affirmations technique.

In Quantum Affirmations, we are learning how to make friends with our subconscious mind, an aspect of ourselves that is not under our conscious control but is as important as our breathing, blood flow, and beating heart, all of which it easily manages (if we are lucky) without a thought from our conscious mind. Our subconscious mind also processes *all* of the information received by our senses and decides what we should pay attention to. This includes our sixth sense, our intuition, which is sometimes fairly screaming at us to not do this or that, or to please do this or that, and which far too many people dismiss as "only" a hunch or that little, easily ignored voice we talk about in hindsight as the part of us we should have listened to but didn't, to our great dismay.

Your subconscious mind also has its ear to your inner thought parade, which is why taking back control of it with my Quantum Affirmations is so important. When you do your quantumplaytion practice well, not just saying it but seeing it and feeling it, too, to your subconscious mind it is almost as if the movie you create in your mind is real. This tells your subconscious mind not only that this is the future that you want to be living in, but also that *you are ready to deal with both the negatives and the positives that are going to be inseparable parts of that reality!*

Your subconscious mind doesn't want you to move into a future that is going to discomfit you, cause you pain, or outright destroy you. As we have already said, that is why you do some of the really weird and apparently self-defeating things you do. To some part of your being, it all makes sense because it is keeping you safe and avoiding the pain you believe you can't handle.

So do you think that this overprotective Jewish mother of a subconscious is going to allow you to become wealthy, to be one of "those people" whom you've told it time and time again you don't like? Do you want to have people looking at you and judging you the way you judge those who now have what you want?

"Let's get real" could be a motto for Quantum Affirmations. If you want to have what you want, if you want it to "get real" in your life so you can enjoy it, then you have to get real, too, about your attitude to the people who have what you want. Prejudice is not just a tragic, stupid waste of time; it is a huge obstacle to your getting what you want. Try being more forgiving and understanding of those who have what you want. Try loving them the way you will want to be loved when you have what you now want—because you're on your way to having it, thanks to the power of your subconscious mind and my Quantum Affirmations technique.

LOVE AND RELATIONSHIPS

I have written a book on the subject of why people don't have the kind of relationships they say that they want to have, *The Soulmate Path*. Earlier, I touched on one of the reasons: not wanting to continue to feel terrible about living alone; that is the real reason so many tell me that they want to meet their soulmate.

Fear of intimacy is another destroyer of relationships, usually before they even get started. I don't mean to dwell on the fact that so many people have incorporated into their inner dialogue the negative voice of everyone who's ever made a critical remark about them, but I have to because so many people literally dwell in that toxic soup of self-criticism. If you have negative feelings about what is going on within you, doesn't it stand to reason that you are going to avoid the possibility of other people, especially other people to whom you are attracted and who you actually want to be with, knowing these deep, dark secrets you hide from the world and maybe even from yourself? It's a double-bind situation: You try to get closer to them, yet you work against yourself in ways you might not even see, trying to push them away and keep your secret self safe in it's aloneness. Even worse, you may find yourself dating or living with someone who is the embodiment of your inner self-critical voice because you believe their criticism to be true and so you enmesh yourself with someone whom you may not really like but who you secretly affirm knows your inner self.

Of course, you may have a myriad of other reasons why you have not found love or why the improvement of your relationships is the goal you now have for your Quantum Affirmations. No one knows you better than you do, if you are honest with yourself. If you come to a particular conclusion as to why you have not found love yet or recently, or why your relationships have suffered, please listen to your heart of hearts. Once you know what obstacles have prevented you from attaining your goal, you have a much better chance of finally reaching it.

WEIGHT LOSS

Everyone knows how to lose weight: Eat fewer calories, control your portions, and get regular exercise that is appropriate for your age, weight, and level of physical fitness. Yet, weight loss is a multibillion-dollar industry. The reason is the same one I've already mentioned a couple of times: Our seemingly crazy behavior makes perfect sense to some aspect of our consciousness.

In business and politics, it is axiomatic that to understand the apparently illogical actions of the various participants, one must "follow the money." By seeing who benefits from what behaviors, a clearer picture eventually emerges.

What benefits does a person derive from being overweight? The most obvious is that eating more than you need to be healthy is a habit, and habits are hard to break. As if that wasn't hard enough to deal with, there are several other benefits to be derived from being overweight.

1. You make yourself unattractive (in your opinion) and thereby give yourself an excuse for not having a relationship or not having a relationship in which you are cherished and loved. You are free to feel isolated from life, just you and your excuses for not plunging in and enjoying life to the full. That doesn't sound like much of a party to me—but to each his or her own.

2. You cushion yourself from life and keep yourself out of the running for the crown in the invisible beauty contest going on in the minds of far too many women and a surprising number of men.

3. You keep yourself from being bothered by men "on the prowl," or even just a threat to friends with relationships, though you should know that if a man likes and feels good being around you, extra pounds are not going to deter his ardor.

4. You are afraid that the change in you that will inevitably come when you lose weight will somehow drive a wedge between you and your friends and, even worse, between you and your loved ones. I know that is a genuine and legitimate fear because I've seen couples go through difficulties when one of them makes a big change like weight loss or sobriety and the other cannot handle the energy that is now free to go into other areas of the relationship.

I still maintain, however, that the truth shall set you free. If you want to lose weight or make any other change in your life, then make it—and let the chips fall where they may. You get only one chance to live your life, and you should do it to the best of your abilities. If someone else cannot handle you at your best, then you are better off without them. Being set free is not without its costs.

CHAPTER 6

STEP THREE

IDENTIFY YOUR GIFT— WHAT FLOWS TO YOU EFFORTLESSLY AND ENDLESSLY?

What flows to and through you both endlessly and effortlessly? This is your gift. You may have only one or you may have many, but always remember that your gift, like what you affirm, is another thing that makes you, you.

Now that you know what you want, why you want it, and a bit about why you haven't gotten it yet, it's time to identify what I call your gift: that which flows to you effortlessly and endlessly. We are going to take your gift and "entangle" it with your goal the way two tiny particles become quantum entangled, forever connected to each other beyond time and space. The object is to have the fearless, doubtless, supremely confident feelings you have about your gift attach themselves to your goal and to remove from your goal as much as possible of the fear you have about it. It may sound complicated, but as you will soon see, it is not. Attaching your gift to your goal is actually a great way to calm yourself down.

What is your gift? What flows to you effortlessly and endlessly? What are you so good at that you simply do it, unafraid, without a shred of doubt that you can do it? It can be anything, really.

One thing most but not all of us are really good at is breathing. Some people struggle for every breath. Becoming aware of your gift gives you self-confidence at the same time that it can and should give you compassion for those less fortunate than you, in terms of their ability to emulate your good fortune with your gift. We all have strengths and weaknesses. The goal is to use our strengths to compensate for our weaknesses and the weaknesses of those we care about. What a wonderful world it would be if this was a universally applied practice.

What are you good at, besides doing negative affirmations so well, of course? It should be something that benefits others, not only you, even if the way others benefit from your gift is by being impressed or otherwise inspired by it. Do you often show kindness, compassion, forgiveness, or love to another person? That is most certainly a gift—and one of the most important. Are you a great spouse, parent, caregiver, friend, student, teacher, co-worker, supervisor, team player, listener, or communicator? Can you fix things, make things, or make things grow? Are you good with children, adults, the elderly, animals, your hands, business, investing, legal matters, law enforcement, investigations, waste management? Are you a good artist, actor, swimmer, singer, designer, diver, cook, wine expert, or dishwasher? No one loads a dishwasher better than me! Are you funny, articulate, a stylish dresser; a good artist, critic, dancer, teacher, musician, DJ, rapper, video-game player; an expert with computers, an athlete, a yogini? Are you a good healer, body worker, pharmacist, bike rider, organizer, leader, politician; highly knowledgeable in math, science, medicine, psychology, finance, systems, drafting, artificial intelligence, nanotechnology, life saving, flying, or philosophizing? You may take your gift for granted, but I hope you will take a moment now to realize that your gift is far from granted to a lot of other people. In fact, it is a good idea to realize that your gift may be another person's goal.

We are often challenged by the duality of life. In the case of Quantum Affirmations, we pursue our goal while being content with what we have because that is the best way to get what we want and enjoy the road to our goal. This duality is quite apparent when we identify our gift. Do not be surprised if, upon identifying your gift, you become aware of the absolute fact that we are each living someone else's dream and someone else's nightmare, and both at the same time.

For example, one of my gifts is that I am a good husband. I am a happily married man who likes nothing better than to be with my wife as much as I can. This is an obvious dream for many, but there are many others who believe with equal conviction that being with the same partner day and night is a nightmare to be avoided at all costs. The same can be said for anything: having children, having a secure career, being famous, living the life of a beach bum—all can be dreams for some and nightmares for others. Even being rich is considered a nightmare for some people, including a surprisingly large group who either have now or have had in the past so much money and so many possessions that their lives became incredibly challenged by the enormous pressures associated with being wealthy—what for so many would seem to be a dream.

Your gift has your unique psychic fingerprints all over it. Honor it. Love it. Do not, however, expect other people to understand how much you love your gift, because they cannot. The important thing is that you do.

Quantum Affirmations

CHAPTER 7

STEP FOUR

ENTANGLE YOUR GIFT WITH YOUR GOAL—WORK YOUR GIFT TO ATTAIN YOUR GOAL

> Here's where the entanglement happens.
> Visualize with certainty a scene in which when you do
> what flows to you endlessly and effortlessly, you also,
> by so doing, attain your goal. For example,
> if you want money or love, you see yourself doing
> what you are good at, and money or love flows
> out of your doing so.

I am delighted to inform you that we have reached the part of my Quantum Affirmations technique where you are ready to start doing some creative visualization. You know what you want and why you want it. You are on to your little inner fear gremlin and why it has been protecting you by keeping you from attaining your goal. You're aware of and thankful for one or more unique gifts that flow to you endlessly and effortlessly. And you're ready to get down to the fun part of Quantum Affirmations.

The most difficult thing about this book is that you occasionally have to stop reading a bit and close your eyes—but not yet! When you do close your eyes, I want you to see yourself working your gift, doing what you do best. See your gift flowing to and through you effortlessly and endlessly. If your gift involves other people, see it flowing to them and see them being made better by it in some way.

There are so many different gifts that you may have that I would never presume to tell you exactly how you should see your gift, but you get the picture, literally. So get the picture in your mind's eye, and when you do, be ready to see a new result come from working your gift.

After you've seen your gift work its magic the way it always does, see the attainment of your goal as a new result of working your gift. If your goal is success as you define it, see yourself doing what you are so good at, your gift, and see a better job, a successful career, fame, power, new abilities, and more flowing to and through you as effortlessly and endlessly as does your gift.

Although Quantum Affirmations is all about saying it, seeing it, and feeling it, I think that someone new to my technique is better off not worrying about saying it for a while. Seeing yourself achieving your goal and feeling what your life will be like when it is real are much more important. By doing that, in effect you will be saying it to yourself in the symbolic language that you use to speak to yourself before you put your thoughts into words. That is the level at which I get my psychic information, and it connects you directly to the most powerful aspects of your being and to reality in general.

So now it's time for me to stop my philosophizing and ask you to please do this exercise, the entangling of your gift with your goal. Once you have created your visualization, I suggest doing it before you go to sleep and upon awakening. You don't have to do it any more than that. Some people enjoy doing it so much that they do it when they get the chance as a sort of brief vacation during the day, especially when they become anxious or aware of the fears that have kept them from their goal. It's totally up to you. As long as you do it twice a day, before sleeping and upon waking before you get out of bed, you are doing it right.

If you can see and feel as real the mental movie of your goal flowing out of and resulting from your doing what flows to you effortlessly and endlessly, you will start to access what I call "the Miracle in Your Mind." This is how we create our reality. Every human-made object around you started off as an idea in someone's mind. The same can be said for all of the scientific knowledge, ideas, laws, political systems, religions, and other tangible effects on reality caused by the human mind. I am not saying that the result of this exercise will be your experience of a reality that matches exactly how you have seen and felt this Miracle in Your Mind. I do believe, however, that it can have a powerful effect on your feelings about the attainment of your goal, especially your fear and anxiety, and thereby empower you to better deal with all aspects of your process.

Quantum Affirmations

CHAPTER 8

STEP FIVE

CREATE A "QUANTUMPLAYTION"— THE MIRACLE IN YOUR MIND

Quantumplaytion is, as I discussed earlier, a play on the word *contemplation*, whose meaning derives from *templum*, the same Latin word from which *temple* originates.

I've already mentioned that the word *templum* meant a space marked out for the Roman official who was responsible for observing and interpreting omens, also known as divination, but I didn't delve into what *divination* really means. Its basic meaning is to "divine," or predict, the future. As a psychic, an expert on astrology and Tarot cards, and the inventor of a series of intuition-building games that help you make better decisions and predict the future, I know a few things about the art of divination.

In my humble opinion, predicting the future is a lot like using an Internet search engine, Google being the one most people are familiar with. When you do an online search, it is an all too rare event to have the information returned to you by the search engine be precisely what you are looking for.

In most cases, you have to refine your search (remember, *if you know your question, you know your answer*), and you have to understand how the search process works and how to interpret the answers you receive.

When you use Tarot cards or astrology or a psychic to help you predict your future, you also have to do a bit of interpretation to get the most out of the answer you receive. I like to think that the process is called "divination" because it helps you access the Divine within us all. I never forget, however, that one of the best ways to predict my own future is to create it myself, both in my mind and in the world, by taking action to realize my goals and not giving up until I do (or until my goals change). This is the essence of and the reason for creating your quantumplaytion.

The reason I asked that you do Step Four, the blending of your gift with your goal, before creating your quantumplaytion is to remove some of the strong, almost magnetic "charge" that is associated with everything that we desire but have not yet attained. This charge is the strongest in those things we feel we desperately need. By blending your gift with your goal, you have made an effort to bring your goal's charge to a much more manageable level. It is now time to make your quantumplaytion in keeping with what you know about your goal, the world, and you.

You can and should produce your quantumplaytion in your mind the way a film editor assembles a movie, and you should do it any way you want to. Accessing your creativity in this way is symbolic of how you are accessing your ability to create your future.

According to the theories of quantum physics, an infinite number of possible futures can be arrived at from actions taken and not taken in the present moment. Many people do not know how a phonograph record works, but allow me to explain the basics of the process because it may help you to understand and visualize yourself arriving at the future you want to get to.

The genius of Thomas Edison invented the phonograph, a device for storing sound waves made in the present moment for future listening. A microphone was invented so that speech and music, as well as the silent absence of both, could be converted into electrical pulses of strengths that were proportional to the volume of the sound. The electrical pulses were fed to a cutting needle that vibrated according to the strength of the pulses and cut into a revolving wax disk a continuous groove that got bigger and smaller according to the way the cutting needle was fed electrical pulses.

After the speech or song was over, the wax disk "master record" containing the continuous groove was used to make a "stamper" that stamped out duplicates of the original wax disk using molten vinyl; these duplicates were sold as phonograph records. The listener would put the phonograph record on the "turn-table," which would spin the record and place at the beginning of the continuous groove a phonograph needle, which would be vibrated by the changes in the record's groove and reverse the original process, sending electrical pulses from the needle's rubbing against the changing groove to an amplifier that would read the pulses and reproduce them as sound through a speaker. Phonograph records we listen to today can faithfully reproduce recording sessions made more than a hundred years ago.

It is as if the present moment is the very sharp tip of a phonograph needle and the record's groove is linear time as we usually conceive of it. But as I said, quantum mechanics states that inherent in every moment are an almost infinite number of possible futures. So reality is like a phonograph record, where the needle rests in a groove, but this groove immediately branches off in an almost limitless number of possible grooves leading to an astounding variety of possible futures. How do we know which branch we will go down?

How can a psychic Tarot-card-reading astrologer like me make any kind of accurate prediction about the future when there are so many possible futures that may arise? That is where the subtle difference between possible futures and probable futures becomes crucial. There is inherent in every moment a more limited set of probable futures, futures that we can logically expect to experience based on present conditions and our reaction to them.

Of course, there is only so much that individuals can do to define and affect and thereby further limit the probable futures they are heading for. One of the main things they can do is to become aware of what they affirm, of what their goal is, and of what their gifts applicable to the attainment of this goal are, and to bring what they affirm and visualize into their consciousness. This, naturally, is my course, my Quantum Affirmations course. When you use my technique, you experience the future you desire twice a day in your mind's eye, and this, at the very least, helps you to clarify your goal and stay focused on achieving it.

Doing your quantumplaytion also entangles your present moment with the probable future you are trying to experience as your reality. Your subconscious mind experiences your quantumplaytion of reality as reality, if you not only say and see it but feel it, too. Having an emotional response in your quantumplaytion is a vital component of the process. The ideal is to experience your quantumplaytion about the situation you are trying to bring into reality the way we experience our dreams, as if they are reality. This is the most practical, results-oriented daydreaming possible to a human being, and I'm proud to be its inventor.

CHAPTER 9

WHAT IS THE SCIENCE UNDERLYING QUANTUM AFFIRMATIONS?

> *Anyone who is not shocked by quantum theory has not understood it.*
>
> —Niels Bohr (1885–1962)

I have been shocked by quantum theory each and every time I've studied it, but I don't think I'll ever claim to understand it. What I do understand, however, is what it's like to be a human being. When you do, you cannot be anything but compassionate and, if you're able, helpful.

I know there is a good chance that many readers might feel cheated if I don't pack this chapter with scientific theories and experiments and the biographies and arguments of the brightest lights of quantum theory (Nobel Prize winner in physics Dr. Bohr, whose quote is at the beginning of this chapter, being one of the brightest). I also know that, after scanning the dry facts and figures of this kind of chapter, almost every single reader would then decide not to read it.

Rather than do all that work for nothing at this time in technological history, the time of the infancy of Internet search-engine technology (with the appropriately baby-talk-sounding Google reigning supreme as of this writing), I will instead put in parentheses the name of the scientific principles I'm writing about, so those interested in learning more can investigate them at their leisure. Instead of boring you with the details, I hope I'm going to inspire you with a few memorable quotes from some of the founders of quantum mechanics and my admittedly unique and controversial take on it.

I'm going to use this chapter as my attempt to dialogue with you, dear reader, my own shocking theories about quantum mechanics and how it allows us to use my Quantum Affirmations technique to change our experience of reality as surely as quantum theory allowed for the design of the semiconductors that power our modern world and the quantum computers that are about to usher in a new age as radically different from today as was the first half of the twentieth century different from the second half, completely transformed, first by the transistor and later by the microchip.

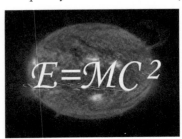

My first bold theory is that the term *New Age* may finally be correctly understood and applied thanks to the strange world of quantum theory, a place where prejudices go to die as surely as did the sickly elephants marching to the elephant graveyard in the old Tarzan movies. What prejudice can withstand the indisputable scientifically proven fact that we are one, that all matter is made of the same stuff, energy? (Look up: Einstein's general theory of relativity, commonly known as $E = mc^2$.)

> *The task is not to see what has never been seen before,*
> *but to think what has never been thought*
> *before about what you see every day.*
>
> —Erwin Schrödinger (1887–1961)

In true dualistic fashion, I find it both hilarious and sadly unscientific that almost all quantum scientists, whose daily work is based on the fact that nothing is certain (look up: the Heisenberg uncertainty principle), are yet certain beyond doubt of the fallacy of seminal ancient New Age principles, such as the principle that we are all one.

I'm not naive, however, and I know that the truly prejudiced will not be swayed by science or other truths. Other truths are my specialty, the New Age kind. I'm such a sensitive New Age guy that I cannot bring myself to dwell on the thought experiment and paradox of quantum physics devised by Schrödinger (look up: Schrödinger's cat) because it involves a possibly dead cat and I love beyond measure our little shaman feline familiar, Zane.

Yet despite my silly unwillingness to sadden myself by dwelling on Zane's mortal nature and the mortal nature of all things, I am big and strong in both body and mind. You have to be if you dare espouse your unique take on any subject, especially astrology, Tarot, psychic phenomena, and the spiritual implications of quantum mechanics. You can get attacked from all sides, the way the various scientists of quantum research did and continue to attack each other's theories. It gets absurd on occasion, with many Tarot card readers thinking astrology is nonsense and vice versa. The degree of vitriol contained in the slings and arrows shot by scientific skeptics, who are really not true skeptics (see T.H. Huxley's quote later in this chapter), about these and all metaphysical and spiritual subjects pales in comparison to some of the barbs loosed by practitioners of one branch of the New Age tree against those of another.

The power of crystals is yet another often derided New Age principle, and it, too, has solid science to validate it. Consider how crucial crystal power is to many of the crowning technological achievements of modern society. Crystals are used to regulate the power of everything from watches to the aforementioned tiny microchips to the massive step-down transformers of transmission power lines. An even more miraculous example of the power of crystals is the ability of electronic devices that contain specially shaped crystals—often rubies—to diffract, internally concentrate, and reflect light in a coherent beam able to travel distances large and small to deliver information or even destructive forces. We call that device a laser, and whole books have been written about how lasers have changed our world. Additionally, a crystal's ability to modulate and control electronic signals and frequencies of all kinds enables radio and television signals, computer chips, and virtually all of our modern communication technologies.

The old saying "Appearances can be deceiving" is true beyond question, a fact with which all quantum researchers and I are in total agreement. A perfect example of this truism is that they and I appear to be on opposite sides of the fence regarding what I consider to be the human application and spiritual New Age implications of quantum theory. The truth of the matter, however, is that we are on the same side of that fence.

Falling back on my tendency for wordplay, rather than use the word *fence*, I should have said that it seems quantum researchers and I are on opposite sides of the double-slit screen used in quantum mechanics' seminal wave/particle duality experiment, the one proving that light can behave as either a particle or a wave, depending upon whether or not the experiment is being observed by someone (look up: wave/particle duality).

The wave/particle duality experiment showed not only that the energy that we call light is able to morph from behaving as a particle to behaving as a wave and back again, but also that the light being used for the slit-screen experiment somehow is conscious of whether or not the process is being observed!

Light is conscious?! Where did I read, "Let there be light?" Light is pure energy, and Einstein proved that all matter is, essentially, energy. In addition to our bodies, human thought—the part of us that is uniquely us—is energy as surely as are the electric currents coursing through our brains' synapses. Might human thought be somehow subject to the proven laws of quantum mechanics? I believe it is, and as you can see, it really is not much of a quantum leap to believe so.

> *I am too much a skeptic to deny the possibility of anything.*
> —Thomas Henry Huxley (1825–1895)

It seems to me that quantum mechanics, if not quantum researchers, has arrived at the same conclusions reached in the universally held ancient shamanic beliefs—affirmations—regarding our true nature, what is commonly called our spirit. This energetic body was also known as our *chi* by the Chinese and was called our *prana* by the Hindus. It can also be called our *vital life force*, our *aura*, or our *etheric body* (*ether* was the medieval alchemists' name for pure energy, unfettered by form, like the *E*, for *energy*, in Einstein's above-mentioned equation, $E = mc^2$!). I will also offer you the notion, heretical to far too many scientists, that quantum mechanics does much to support the fundamental tenets of all religions, at least those based on the oneness of all and the kindness to all that logically follows from that affirmation.

I have become increasingly disappointed in the harsh tone used these days by those who disagree with one another, usually online and anonymously. The harshest criticism seems to be reserved for astrologers, Tarot readers and psychics; it is the last bastion of acceptable prejudice. You will never find me deriding a single pseudo-skeptic or quantum researcher for being unaware of how contrary to the most basic and proven tenets of quantum mechanics is their certainty that spirituality and the energy of the human mind are not inextricably intertwined with the same laws that govern the waves and particles of energy underlying all matter. I forgive them because they apparently know not what they do. If they do know it and still deride my take on the intersection of the New Age with the quantum age, then they are no longer scientists and so fair game for my derision.

The man who cannot occasionally imagine events and conditions of existence that are contrary to the causal principle as he knows it will never enrich his science by the addition of a new idea.

—Max Planck (1858—1947)

I don't know whether this book and my Quantum Affirmations will one day be acknowledged as one of the foundational works on the long-needed meeting of science and matters of the spirit, the way Max Planck is acknowledged as being the founder of quantum theory. All I or anyone knows without doubt is the apparent existence of oneself as a unique being as evidenced by the thought parade of various affirmations coursing through our consciousness, the same one that we are working to influence by creating our Quantum Affirmations and quantumplaytions.

The fact that within these pages we are working at the very doors of perception and reality, including the very creation and re-creation of both, was often overwhelming to me during the writing of this book. I wrote this chapter last because I have so much respect for you and the pioneers of quantum mechanics that I wanted to be sure that I got it right before I presented it to you as worthy of your consideration and time. I have never been more satisfied with a book I've written, and I doubt I ever will be, though a good quantum "mechanic" should always be comfortable with uncertainty.

The remainder of this book contains both my modest foray into scientific experiment and some seemingly magical tools I've used to change my own life.

The science is in the next four chapters, which contain conversations I had with people in which I explained and practiced a full-blown Quantum Affirmation, as well as a follow-up conversation that examined their progress six and then twelve weeks later. Please read through all of them because although I have given you a basic understanding of my Quantum Affirmations theory, I have not yet given you all the information you need to properly design and do your own Quantum Affirmations. I affirm beyond doubt that the best way for you to complete your understanding of my technique and be able to apply it in the real world is to listen in on these four sessions.

I've placed the magical tools in the two chapters following the four conversations. In Chapter 14 you will find my six Q-U-A-N-T-U-M rules for increasing the effectiveness of your practice and in Chapter 15 the thirty-six Quantum Aspirations, supercharged affirmations for you to use when daily life seems like it is trying to scientifically prove that you can't do this or that, that all your critics were right, and that all of my Quantum Affirmations techniques are "mere fantasy." When that happens—and happen it will—you may also want to remember the following quote from the most reluctant believer of the several founders of quantum mechanics.

> *When I examined myself and my methods of thought,*
> *I came to the conclusion that the gift of fantasy*
> *has meant more to me than my*
> *talent for absorbing positive knowledge.*
>
> —Albert Einstein

Four Real-Life Quantum Affirmations Success Stories:
THE DIALOGUES

The world-famous dialogues by the Greek philosopher Plato (ca. 428–348 BCE), student of Socrates (ca. 470–399 BCE) and teacher to Aristotle (ca. 384–322 BCE; himself the teacher of Alexander the Great), are one of the seminal works of Western philosophy. Of course, Plato's dialogues were based on the conversations of people arguing various philosophies, mainly with Socrates, while mine are simply a record of me working one-on-one with four wonderful people who volunteered to give my Quantum Affirmations technique a try over a period of twelve weeks.

I humbly submit the following dialogues with the hope that they, too, can empower you to think more clearly, make better choices, and lead a more fulfilling life. I found to my surprise that these sessions, video recorded originally for the exclusive One Spirit Book Club edition (for information on the DVD and the CD of guided Quantum Affirmations, see the About the Author chapter on page 198), were not only an exploration and a confirmation of the power of the Quantum Affirmation techniques I'd evolved in my own life; they brought the whole system to a new level. I came to realize that they must become the central focus of this book.

Each person's dialogue centers around one of the four subjects that have been and continue to be the most important to my clients.

- Success

- Wealth

- Love

- Weight loss

With cameras rolling, we sat together and got down to the important business of Quantum Affirmations. You will see that although each person came with one of the four major themes uppermost in his or her mind, we *invariably* found that other issues were equally important to the clarification and attainment of each person's original goal. I knew I could not adequately explain this phenomenon to you by simply relating the story in my own words; you have to experience these dialogues to watch the process unfold. Not only are they interesting and often humorous, but each one provides a road map into the Quantum Affirmations landscape that I know you will find valuable as you embark on your own journey to the life you've always wanted to live.

CHAPTER 10

CASE STUDY

QUANTUM AFFIRMATION FOR SUCCESS— MICHELE AND JOYCE

All honest work is noble and can be a source of pride. Even if the reason you're reading *Quantum Affirmations* is to manifest a better job or embark on the career you've always dreamed about, it is a good idea to prepare yourself for this chapter and your new life by first acknowledging the good things about your present situation. Take a moment to recognize the positive things—even just one positive thing—about your current situation.

We are, each of us, beautiful souls with senses of humor, even if that beauty and humor are hidden beneath hard layers of protective beliefs and behaviors designed to keep us from getting hurt. Acknowledging the things that are good and noble about our present situation helps us to feel good about ourselves, or at least a little less self-critical, and that puts us in a better frame of mind for doing our Quantum Affirmations and manifesting the improvements we desire to see in our lives.

Unless we are either very fortunate or very unfortunate, most of us spend the majority of our waking lives occupied by our work, whether we think of that work as "just" a job or as a full-blown career. The origin of the word *career* reveals the difference between the two. It can be found in the Latin word *carraria*, meaning a vehicular road upon which a "carrus," a wagon, can travel.

Wagons and roads are for people on the move. They're for hauling from place to place all the countless things that create and sustain civilization. Our career is the road that we travel in life. Even the word *career* seems to imply work that takes us on a journey, while the word *job* seems attached to a place with far fewer opportunities for any kind of advancement.

In fact, the very word *job* may be derived from the obsolete English word for *lump*. I'm not saying that everyone who has a job sits there like a lump. And I won't make the obvious comparison of a job we do not enjoy to the suffering of the biblical patriarch Job, who was sorely tested by Jehovah. The main contrast has to do with a job being simply a piece of work done for pay and a career, which has a goal and a road to take you there.

The first dialogue is with Michele, and it describes the Quantum Affirmations approach to first defining and then creating your definition of success. As an added bonus I've also included at the end of this chapter a letter I received from Joyce detailing how her Quantum Affirmations practice helped her. If my Quantum Affirmations technique helps you achieve a particular goal, not just success, please write to me using my contact information that is contained in the About the Author chapter on page 198. I'd love to hear from you.

Michele: Before

MONTE: The first thing we do when activating the power of my Quantum Affirmations technique is to identify our goal. What future do you want to step into? That's the reality we are going to experience in our "quantumplaytion," our Quantum Affirmations–powered visualization. The clearer you can see this future, the sooner and surer it becomes the probable future, which can then become your new reality. So when I say to you, "Identify your goal," what comes to mind?

MICHELE: Well, I think that question is asking me to get to the root of what I really want, because I have so many different interests and I've done lots of different things, but nothing is really fueling my passion.

MONTE: I think that's it for most people. When we're talking about work or career, we're really talking about what makes you feel passionate and alive and fulfills your purpose. I'm always surprised when people talk about the "mystery" regarding the purpose or the meaning of life. I have always thought that the purpose of my life is to give my life purpose and the meaning of life is to make sure that my life has meaning.

MICHELE: Yes. I have a lot of interests and I have a lot of talents, but it seems I can't really combine and focus them in one direction. It's like having the ingredients to make a cake—I have the eggs, I have the butter—but being unable to put the cake together. I have all the ingredients, but I don't like the recipe or I don't even like having to put it in the oven, so I feel like I'm always half-baked. *(Laughter)*

MONTE: In your case, I think we're going to have to go on to the second step in my Quantum Affirmations technique to get back to the first step. The first step is identifying your goal. The second step is identifying your gifts. By gifts, I mean what flows effortlessly and endlessly to you. Your gifts are anything that you don't worry about, something that you have no doubts about, the way you have regarding your search for success. In terms of the goal you've come here to work on attaining, what is something that you're completely passionate about?

MICHELE: Well, when I think about what I spend a lot of time on because I want to, then that would have to be metaphysics. Yes, I spend a lot of time on things in that realm.

MONTE: Is the reason that you don't focus on or have a passion for any one particular thing because it doesn't seem that metaphysics enters into this particular aspect of life that you're talking about?

MICHELE: Well, I've been trying to figure out how to incorporate it into my life with my involvement in the fashion and beauty industry.

MONTE: That flows pretty endlessly and effortlessly to you, right? The fashion and the beauty?

MICHELE: Yes. Well, it flows, but then there's a wall. I always hit a wall.

MONTE: But if someone comes to you and wants to look their best, do you ever think to yourself, *Uh-oh, here it is. This is a person I can't help.* Or do you just know that, no matter who comes to you, you can make them look fabulous? If budget is not an issue, you can certainly do it, right?

MICHELE: Oh yes, I can definitely make them look their best, but you know what always comes to mind? I can make them look right, but it actually always feels so superficial. I always feel, later on, when I see them again, like I failed them in some way because I don't feel like they really are empowered. I just feel like I put a Band-Aid on whatever it is that's troubling them. I work with women all the time, and sometimes they are really very beautiful, very prosperous, and they seem like they have it all. They get a new outfit from me, and the next time I see them they want another new outfit. The one they just got from me isn't doing it for them anymore—it's like they're never satisfied. I often laugh about it after, and I think I helped them, but deep down I know it isn't funny; it isn't right.

MONTE: You worry that you sort of enabled their addiction?

MICHELE: Yes. Even the times when I thought that we connected and that I helped them, I often come to believe that I
really did not, that they're still stuck where they were.

MONTE: Right. But since they didn't come to you to get
unstuck, there's only so much you can do. To get well, a
person has to at least know that they're sick.

MICHELE: I've tried to work from a standpoint of trying to give
them something mentally as well as something physically to
put on.

MONTE: Reviving them at the same time. But, once again,
there's only so much you can do since they came to you specifically for your expert beauty advice.

MICHELE: Yes, and I think that's what makes me feel like this
is just really so superficial. I think, *Should I really be doing this?*
(Laughter)

MONTE: Because you don't feel like they're living up to your
highest ideals for them and you're not living up to your highest ideals for what you should be doing with your life.

MICHELE: Yes.

MONTE: You say you feel like you're putting a Band-Aid on a
wound. It says in the Bible that Jesus said, "Behold, I stand at
the door, and knock: if any man hear my voice, and open the
door, I will come in to him, and will sup with him, and he
with me." What I get from that is that you have to invite truth
into your life. I mean, you're here and we're talking about

this issue because you're ready to talk about it. Those women are not necessarily ready to talk about it or possibly are not ready to talk about it with you. Many people are not comfortable speaking about their inner thoughts and behavior with anyone, not even themselves.

I think that might be the issue; you're judging yourself harshly because you're not able to help them break through their self-imposed limitations. You are in a position to give them good advice, but you're not doing so for a very logical reason: because you're not there as an adviser; you're there as a sales associate for the most prestigious specialty store in the world, whose management doesn't want you to do anything with its customers except what you're paid for—sell things to them. So maybe that's what your passion is—counseling, teaching, and advising people. Perhaps your quantumplaytion visualization should be to put yourself in a position where you're a spiritual teacher since you've obviously studied it long enough to know a lot.

MICHELE: You guys are my superheroes. *(Laughter)* And the interesting thing about meeting you and Amy is that I think I'm attracted to you guys because you are mixing art with metaphysics and fashion. *(Amy's Spiritual Couture™ one-of-kind evening jackets, caftans, robes, and jewelry have been sold exclusively at Bergdorf Goodman in New York City for more than twelve years.)* You have all the energies that I'm attracted to. I found you without even meeting you on the Internet, and then I…

MONTE: Metaphysically.

MICHELE: Metaphysically. And then I met you . . .

MONTE: Like we were fated to meet. Exactly. But I also think the reason that you're attracted to us is that we're not full of it and that we're keeping it real.

MICHELE: Yes, exactly.

MONTE: I think that if we're going to do a Quantum Affirmation about you doing your version of what we do, that might be the issue, because I'm sure that, like us, you've met people who pretend to be doing the metaphysical and the spiritual, and a lot of them were talking the talk but stumbling and falling when they tried to walk the walk.

MICHELE: Exactly. Well, I've had an experience like that.

MONTE: Yes, we all have.

MICHELE: And then I just decided, well, maybe I don't want to do this.

MONTE: But the more important thing is that you can vow to be one of the different ones; you can keep it real. It should be easier for you because you know us and you have seen that we have done it and we know you can do it, too. I mean, it's a free-flowing thing. You and the other people who know and love the work we've been doing through our books since 1988 help us to feel good about ourselves—that helps us deal with the rejections and other difficulties that are part of even a blessed life like the one we've been enjoying for so long. On a metaphysical level, one of the reasons that Amy and I exist is to help people feel good about themselves, and not just with our books and art and fashions and jewelry, but every time we meet up with anyone. So you have to put yourself in a situation where you can share your spiritual knowledge and your gifts with those who come to hear it, if that is your Quantum Affirmation. You can have a completely different one, of course, either instead of or in addition to that one, but that seems to be at the core of what I hear you saying.

MICHELE: I think that we're definitely hitting upon something, because it's been hovering around me for years, and I feel that—the reason why I came up with this is that I'm trying to look at what I spend most of my time doing. Those areas should be what I'm passionate about, right?

MONTE: That's a good way to get there.

MICHELE: I thought, well, I'm not looking at fashion Web sites; I don't look at magazines. I'm always looking for new spiritual books and magazines to read at Barnes and Noble and for Tarot card decks and books about the power of crystals and stones. I think maybe that's my interest because I spend a lot of my time doing that.

MONTE: Well, then, that's your passion—no doubt about it.

MICHELE: And then when people ask me about the latest fashion blog, I'm, like, "Oh, I don't know." *(Laughter)*

MONTE: That flows so effortlessly and endlessly that you know you don't have to worry about it, right?

MICHELE: When it comes to style and beauty and fashion, it's more of an intuitive thing with me. I've been that way my whole life.

MONTE: Right. Someone else would love to have that fashion-sense gift of yours. Everyone has a different gift, if they'll just calm down, stop worrying and doubting, and take a dispassionate look at themselves—that means no self-criticism for a couple of minutes!

MICHELE: I do my own personal fashion, and the guidance I give to women at the store I do intuitively, but when it comes to metaphysical and spiritual pursuits, I'm always exploring. So when you asked me the question, I thought, *Well, what do I spend most of my time doing when I'm at home, my downtime?* Just before, I was sitting in the other room waiting for you guys to be ready for me, and I was looking at some of the books and games you've done—I didn't know you've done *that* many! I thought, yes, maybe that combination of spirituality and practicality that you combine in your books, your careers, and your personal lives could definitely work for me.

MONTE: I think we're making some really good progress here.

MICHELE: Yes.

MONTE: Because one of the reasons we're writing *Quantum Affirmations* and making this DVD is to help other people find out exactly what it is that they want out of life, on the spiritual, mental, and physical levels, and not only the metaphysical level. We know beyond doubt that spirituality is creativity and that it is a very practical thing, too. You have to grasp on to the spirit of anything that you want to make manifest in the world, whether that's a new job or a new identity.

Getting back to your specific situation, it's obvious that you love to help people; that's what I'm hearing. What you're looking for when you're searching on the Internet and reading all these things is your particular take on all these things. And I'll bet you're not finding it, so that may be where you're going—getting out to the world your unique take on how spirituality can be applied to daily life.

MICHELE: Exactly.

MONTE: Because I think you've been doing it. From what I know about you, you've been doing it long enough that you could tell people what you know, what you've experienced in your interesting life. You don't have to do it for fifty years before you tell people. If you've studied it for five years or ten years, you could tell someone who is just getting into it about your personal take on the subject, and it can be very useful because you still have the Zen mind, the childlike beginner's mind that assumes nothing and questions everything (within reason). You can help the person who is first getting into what you have experience with because you remember what it's like to be at the beginning and what it feels like to not know.

MONTE: This is one of the most important things about Quantum Affirmations—trying to figure out what it is that you want. And I love the fact that we're not rushing the process and worrying about zeroing in on anything in particular, because I think now we're really going to help people, since most people are like this. They don't know exactly what it is that they want; they don't even know exactly what they *could* want—what's possible for them to experience in this life.

It is always important to realize that when you talk about moving toward and into the probable future you desire, you are talking about profoundly changing your life. Do you want to change your life? Do you want things to be different?

MICHELE: Most definitely. I mean, I can get totally depressed about it; I sometimes think I'm in purgatory. *(Laughter)*

MONTE: Okay, so how would you like things to be different? By the way, that's pretty brave of you to say that you are sometimes depressed and feel like you're in purgatory. Honesty is always the best policy, especially with oneself. You can't get where you're going if you don't know or won't admit where you are and where you've been.

MICHELE: Yes, I think I can see things differently. Besides wanting to do work that I feel passionate about, I have to admit that I feel myself wanting more security now, more financial security.

MONTE: Yes, especially now. It is hard to find what helps you to feel more secure in the best of economic times, and these times are far from that. It's a real Depression for so many people, even if the government and the mainstream media don't want to tell it like it is.

But despite the economic despair, some people are doing all right, and there's no reason you cannot be one of them. You have to know that you're getting enough material things—money, clothes, a nice place to live, transportation, luxuries—none of that takes anything away from anyone else. There's enough for everyone, metaphysically and from a Quantum Affirmations perspective. As a kind person, it is crucial that you know this is true, or else your powerful subconscious won't let you acquire more for fear that you're depriving someone less fortunate than you.

What else would you like to experience in your life? You don't have to limit what you want as long as what you want is within reason.

MICHELE: I know I need more grounding, because I don't think I'm really grounded.

MONTE: Okay. Quantum Affirmations can help you take yourself to the probable future where you have all of those things and more, if you can identify them, and you apparently can!

MICHELE: Definitely more of a lifestyle that I enjoy, things that I like to do, like actually being immersed in the things I love versus always trying to look for things to do in the hope that I'll find "the big thing" I like to do the most and get paid for it. I'm always thinking, *Oh, maybe that's something that I'd like to do.* I'm always experimenting with different things. I'll go to different art shows. I'll listen to different types of music. I like a very eclectic lifestyle, but I feel like I'm all over the place.

MONTE: But it sounds like you're leading the lifestyle of an arts critic. It is important that we rise above all of our "stuff"—our self-criticisms and limiting beliefs about what is possible for us—and look to see if, from that higher perspective, any patterns are emerging. When we do this, we can better envision a job or career that can encompass all of our passions, if that is at all possible. If not, we have to do our best and set our Quantum Affirmations with a goal of coming up with a job or career that contains one or more of our passions. In any event, we must find the good in where we are now and build on it. If we have come this far, we can go even farther.

We are powerful beings. We can even invent a new job or career! These days, with so many technological advancements and yet so many people out of work, we are seeing more and more people use their creativity by creating new ways of earning a living. You may evolve a new definition for the term *arts critic*.

MICHELE: That's very interesting that you say that.

MONTE: Well, ideally you're going to a future where you make your living from doing all the things that interest you, or at least that's the goal we're going to strive for.

MICHELE: That's very spot-on, and I'm going to tell you why.

MONTE: Okay, I am pleased but not surprised. After all, I am psychic. *(Laughter)*

MICHELE: Because recently I met a woman who teaches at Juilliard. We were discussing the arts. She's an actress and she's an older woman, and she said, "You know what? The world needs more art critics," and she specifically said art critics of color. *(Michele is an American of African descent.)* She went into this whole thing while I was, at the same time, listening to my friend Chris recite, because I was actually there, at this event, writing a story about him as a poet. When she said this to me, I said, "Really?"

Lately I've been given all these different writing assignments. Over the last year, people have said that they like my writing. I had never thought of myself as being a writer, so when you said art critic, this is the third time this week I've heard *art critic* as a career for me to consider pursuing.

MONTE: With Quantum Affirmations, it is crucial that you first determine what you want to do. If you don't know, then your Quantum Affirmation should be that you will soon arrive at the probable future where you know what it is that you are passionate about and what you would like to experience as your line of work or career.

Now, *art critic*; is that something you might want to do for a while? Nothing says you have to pick any one thing and do only that for the rest of your life. Experimentation is fine, just as long as you are practical and don't do anything that causes you to be without money. It sounds like you're living the life of an art critic anyway, so you might as well get paid for it.

MICHELE: Well, yes, that's very interesting. You definitely have sparked something.

MONTE: What would be the negative, problematic things that would come with being an art critic?

My Quantum Affirmations technique requires that you embrace both the positive and the negative things that will come with your new reality. Whatever it is that you desire, whatever changes you want to see in your daily experience of life, there are going to be negative, problematic situations that arise along with your new reality. No matter how positive you think your new life will be, how pleasurable, it is vitally important to your Quantum Affirmations practice that you admit that there are negative things about it, too.

So, let's examine the positives and negatives of being an art critic. First of all, getting paid for such work is hard.

MICHELE: Yes.

MONTE: I don't know if that would fit in with your desire for stability. As I said, I never, ever thought I'd be a writer of books and an inventor of games that teach you astrology and how to read Tarot cards and how to predict the future, and yet that's exactly what I've done. When I started doing it I was told by someone who I loved and respected that there was no way to make a living doing it, and, though she was correct in that it is not an easy task, that is exactly the future that Amy and I went on to create. We have not only made a living; we have made a life for ourselves—and a body of work that will live on when our bodies die.

They don't tell people when they're growing up, "You could be an arts critic"—and I'm saying *arts*, with an *s*—but it sounds like that's what your life is all about. Since it sounds like you really don't like to get bored, then let's say for the moment that it's an arts critic's life for you. I hear that you don't want to be a music critic because then you always have to listen to music. You want it all, including the experimental stuff that defies categories.

MICHELE: Exactly.

MONTE: You want to go to everything, every performance, every show. You want to go to the interesting places and meet the interesting people. Even though this is work that most people are not interested in doing, it applies to everyone because each of us is doing a job that a lot of other people are not interested in doing.

So then the next thing would be—if we were doing Quantum Affirmations with the goal being to bring you to the probable future where you are an art critic—we can start with the most obvious negatives of the difficulty in getting a job as an arts critic. I don't mean just blogging or otherwise giving your work away for free, which would not satisfy your desire for security, but getting paid for doing it. If you can do your Quantum Affirmations on a regular basis, it sounds like you can get paid for work that you're passionate about.

The great thing to realize when you're doing Quantum Affirmations is that when you get to your goal, it doesn't mean you can't have other goals. This is just one goal we're talking about, and there are always going to be more. That's the nature of the human condition.

I often do readings for people with millions of dollars. They, too, have wants and needs and desires and problems. Many of these problems are identical to the problems we have—worries about love and money and family and work and losing weight. Of course, the particulars of many of their problems are very different because, let's face it, money often changes everything in a person's life—having it and not having it—which is why it is a major issue for almost everyone. But still virtually all the problems of daily life are basically the same for everyone, rich or poor or in between, only originating from a different kind of starting point.

So to do a Quantum Affirmation–powered quantumplaytion about you getting paid to be an arts critic, then we'd have to apply all your passions, including your passion to help people to identify their own passion, as one of the facets of the jewel of a life you're creating for yourself, with or without my Quantum Affirmations technique. My technique helps you get there a lot faster and a lot more easily because it is designed to help a person become crystal clear about where they want their life to go. I don't know how people expect to get to a better life for themselves without a clear picture of where they are going.

MICHELE: I'm thinking as I'm sitting here listening to you. Something came to mind because I can see how everything that I do is based on how it affects the human condition, as you said. So basically with the arts, with clothing, the question for me now is, How is it going to make someone feel better? What does it do to their spirit and how is it actually affecting their psyche? Is it going to make you feel good or is it disturbing?

I once met someone who actually is in the art world and we were walking through a gallery, and I thought, *This makes no sense. Why did this person make this?* And my friend said, "It's all about the fact that you're feeling something when you look at it, whether pleasure or disgust or indifference, and that's what makes things change in the art world. It's the emotional response to things."

And so as we were speaking, I was thinking, *Oh, well, maybe that's why people enjoy my writing, because I'm always writing from the aspect of feelings and empowerment and thinking, How is this going to affect the people who read it?* When I look at Amy's work, I think about how amazing it must be to choose the fabrics and put the piece together, thinking about what it means and the energy it creates. So I'm looking at everything from the energy standpoint when I look at art, at clothing. I love the way this is starting to become clear to me—so maybe as you're saying this to me I'm getting this vision, these pictures of me as an arts critic—maybe that's the story of my life for a while?

MONTE: It certainly seems like it is the story, and it's a unique story, too. Your gift and your goal are so right there in front of you that it's like water is to a fish; you're in it so much that you don't see it or see that you're in it; it's just you. Many people don't realize that they can actually earn a living doing what they enjoy doing. It's like the great title of that book, *Do What You Love, The Money Will Follow*. It's not just wishful thinking. My Quantum Affirmations is my way of proving that is true.

MICHELE: Even so, sometimes I just feel like I'm all over the place in my head. I feel like I'm here and there and everywhere all at the same time.

MONTE: But you're not; you're really not. Your Quantum Affirmation is right here. It's really not in the future, and this is a very interesting…I'm not going to call it a case. *(Chuckles)*

MICHELE: Case study?

MONTE: It's a case study. *(Laughter)* This is fascinating to me because we're doing it right here, right now, no planning, just being as honest as we can with each other and with ourselves. I mean, this is so very in the moment; using the Quantum Affirmations process is getting us closer and closer to your goal. It is not unusual for a person to come to me thinking that they want "that" and, after drilling down to the heart of the matter, to find that they want something else instead.

I keep coming back to your desire for security. Even though this book is about getting what you want, it is important to remember that, no matter what any of us has as our experience of life in this moment, we can only *feel* secure; we can never actually *be* secure. I laugh when I hear people talking about having "unreasonable expectations." *All* expectations are unreasonable because no one is guaranteed another breath, let alone winning the lottery. I say this as someone who has as many unreasonable expectations as anyone else. I couldn't write this book or do anything else without expecting things, but I try to be aware of as much truth about life as I can be because I do believe that the truth shall set me free. Denying this or any other truth and trying to bury it only makes you anxious and fearful, because running from something tells your subconscious that you are afraid; you cannot handle it. Since our subconscious wants us to realize our potential, it then works to bring into our life again and again what we are afraid of until we rise to the occasion and deal with what we're afraid of.

MICHELE: That's certainly been true in my life.

MONTE: Mine, too! Getting back to your unique situation, to me one of the main arts of being a working artist is getting paid for it, unless you are independently wealthy or unless you're doing it as a hobby.

You, Michele, are so into what you're doing already, you're doing it now. All you have to do is add to your mix of writing what you see and writing what you feel the image of seeing yourself getting paid for it. The thing with Quantum Affirmations is that you never have to say to the future, "This is exactly how it's going to happen."

If you're going to be an art critic, you're going to be an art critic. Let magic happen. The way it's going to happen is going to blow your mind and it's going to blow my mind, because the universe always does it in a way that is mind-blowing. Yes, it sounds like you're in it. You've just got to gather it all up and take it someplace and get paid for it.

MICHELE: I had to come to East Hampton. *(Laughter)*

MONTE: A big part of Quantum Affirmations is to remember that sometimes you have to step out of yourself to step into yourself. My technique requires that relentless, *Oh yes? Well what about…?* I'm talking about questioning yourself and what you are affirming thoroughly. We are all quite creative at avoiding looking at what we affirm and do and say with a dispassionate, critical though loving eye. We have to see ourselves as children, sweet, innocent, and desiring to learn.

It sounds like you're really there because you're passionate about living your life so that it's unfettered, so that no one is telling you that you have to do the same thing every day.

MICHELE: Yes.

MONTE: You have to be able to go to this party or to go to this art opening. I don't even think it's all about the parties with you. I think it's that you want to go to the place where the music's happening or the art is happening.

MICHELE: Yes. I want to go to the place where I think life as we know it and what is possible is changing, interesting. It doesn't necessarily have to be popular. It just has to be some kind of movement.

MONTE: Well, yes, as long as you remember writer Ernest Hemingway's admonishment to actress Marlene Dietrich: "Never confuse movement with action."

MICHELE: Yes.

MONTE: Reporting about what's going on culturally can certainly be a great way to earn a living. I once read that in the early years of television, *TV Guide* magazine made more money than was made by all the programs on television because people were willing to pay to find out what was on and what *TV Guide*'s critics thought about each show. The information about the information was more valuable than the information. You're an art critic.

MICHELE: Okay.

MONTE: Nobody makes you an art critic. No one says you're an art critic. You are and you don't need anybody to tell you what you are, especially if you are using my Quantum Affirmations technique. Outwardly, your work and career are quite different from how most people earn a living, but the essential facts are the same. We affirm certain things about life and what we want to do with our time to earn a living. No one can tell us what that is; they can only show us possibilities to actualize our being. When you are using the Quantum Affirmations technique, you join them in showing yourself possibilities that you might otherwise not even consider.

In that way, you've been living the life of an arts critic and you don't need anybody to give to you assignments. You are the art critic who the artists are not afraid to see show up at their art event because they know you're not going to just be vicious and you're not writing to hear your voice. You're writing to help people, with love, and if you're going to criticize anything in that kind of traditional criticism, it would be to make it better for them the next time. I know you; I know that's how you would write it.

MICHELE: Yes, that's very true, because that's what I do when I meet people; I always say, "Wow, this is really nice. Have you thought about doing this?" I'm always thinking about what they can do to make what they're doing more interesting, more in line with what they say they're trying to do.

MONTE: Right, and people will listen to what you say because you have a great look, a great way to present yourself. You look like you have it all together and don't need anything from anyone. You're a Leo rising, right? When Leo-rising people walk into the room, everyone turns around. The negative to being a Leo rising is that since you have such a strong, proud presentation of yourself, no one will feel sorry for you or offer to help you. They'll listen to you, however, because as a Leo rising you look like an actress or a performer. Leo is all about performing, and so the Quantum Affirmation for you in the moment is actually going back to the New York City area and being an art critic.

MICHELE: Just doing it, making it real.

MONTE: Making it real and getting paid for it, really. I don't mean to sound overly focused on money. I am aware that when you're talking about what you are passionate about, you don't even have to get paid for it. I was a performing singer-songwriter, and the club owners know that you'll do it for free, so they want you to play for the "exposure." I used to tell them, "You know, people can die from exposure." So I'm like one of those club owners; I know you'll do it even if you don't get paid.

MICHELE: But I want to get paid for it *(Laughter)* because that's part of my Quantum Affirmation, too. That's a very cool part of the affirmation—getting paid for doing things.

MONTE: Close your eyes. Know that you're an art critic. It's on your business card, your mental business card. See someone saying, "What do you do?" and you replying to them, "I'm an art critic." That's what you do. You're now an art critic. See yourself as you write your blog, you write your e-mails, you write your newspaper column, you go on camera for a video blog, a TV show, radio, Internet—you can do it all.

You can do it any way you want and know that the money will come and you don't have to know how it will come. The quantumplaytion is to see the checks coming in the mail because you're not going to go to an office and you're not going to work for a particular person. So to see the checks coming in—and what's the negative with that? The negative is you're an art critic and now you have to be able to...*(Laughter)* You have to be able to stand up...

MICHELE: Now I have to do it.

MONTE: Well, first, you have to do it, and we've just seen in your mind's eye you doing exactly that. But, second, when you walk in the room and they know you're an art critic, it's like when you're a food critic: The people working and owning the restaurant all go nuts when a food critic goes into their restaurant. Quantum Affirmations is all about the bright light and the shadow. The bright light is what you want. The shadow is what comes with the territory, and there's always a shadow side to things, even with being an art critic. You're Michele H., art critic. It's exciting.

Creating your quantumplaytion is always a bit like putting on a play, whether you're doing it alone or with me or one of the teachers I train—you can certainly be one of them! There's always a bit of "stage fright" involved because you are, in essence, acting. Every actor experiences stage fright, but most of them enjoy it the way people who like roller coasters and horror movies enjoy those scary experiences.

MICHELE: I just got "style critic" instead of arts critic.

MONTE: It's your life. I think that style critic is fine because everything and everyone has style.

MICHELE: I think style critic. We're definitely having a break-through.

MONTE: Yes.

MICHELE: I know that I'm feeling it. I'm getting that buzz in my ear.

MONTE: And it's passion.

MICHELE: It's this tingle that you get, like a buzz. It's an awakening kind of thing. I definitely feel like we've broken through something. I was feeling the path developing and I've been trying to figure out this thing in my writing, and you saying everything you've said today…everything's kind of pulling together. Even people; I keep meeting a lot of artists—that I'm helping. I tell them, "Well, I'll do that for you." I'll read something that they've written to promote themselves and I'll say, "You know what? I'll just rewrite this for you."

MONTE: That's great.

MICHELE: And they say, "You will? Really?" And then I'll rewrite it and they tell me that they really like it.

MONTE: We're doing the real heavy lifting, removing the barriers to you seeing what you're passionate about and what you can do to earn your living that can incorporate that for you.

MICHELE: Yes.

MONTE: I mean, this is the real work. This is the real stuff. We're in East Hampton, out on Long Island. We're in the Springs area of East Hampton, and Jackson Pollock died at the end of our street. The great Willem de Kooning lived around the corner from us. He used to sit on our front lawn when Amy's father was alive.

MICHELE: Wow!

MONTE: Neither of those Abstract Expressionist artists would be who they were if it wasn't for Clement Greenberg and art critics like him because they needed people who were in the position to say, "Look, everyone, I say this artist is important. You should know about this. Don't miss the boat; be the first to know what's new and good, and that is going to have an effect on the culture." Back then there weren't too many venues to get that message out. Today, there are hundreds of them, but I'd like to think that the cream will always rise to the top of the milk; what's good and especially what's great, like Amy's fabric collage tapestries, will be acknowledged as an important part of our culture, about what's good about our culture, I mean.

MICHELE: This is really something. I just got another chill *(Laughter)* because I'm reading about this artist, a woman. She totally is living in obscurity right now and her name is Betty Davis and she's a black woman who was like a rock star of an artist from the seventies. She actually used to hang out with Jimmy Hendrix.

MONTE: My turn to say "Wow!"

MICHELE: She just wrote this whole story. She's living in poverty right now. She should've been one of the biggest stars ever, and I was just reading her notes on the train coming up here about her life and how she was so ahead of her time that she's living in poverty right now. I thought this is so sad because she's so talented and if I'd been writing about her, like I wrote in my blog...

I've introduced people to her over the last week, and they've said, "I've never heard of her." She's like Lady Gaga, her costumes; everything about her was so ahead of her time. When you said that, I'm thinking, yes, she would be a bigger star if she had someone who really wrote about her.

MONTE: That's true.

MICHELE: And there are so many people like that.

MONTE: In the book *Gulliver's Travels* by Jonathan Swift, the king had these people called flappers, and their job was to flap the king's ear when there was something he should listen to. The critics are the flappers. They flap the public's ear because there are a billion blogs, there are a billion art shows, everyone's got Adobe Photoshop, and we're all so busy and pulled in so many directions. We need someone who we respect, whose taste we respect, who will point us to where the important work is being done. We need a really good guide to the right stuff, and I think that that's what we've arrived at here.

The Quantum Affirmation–powered quantumplaytion for you is different than for most people. Most people are not already doing so much of what they want to be doing. Your challenge is really to live as a style critic while using the quantumplaytion technique to visualize yourself getting paid for it. It's not really necessarily for you to reinvent yourself; you just need to rework how you think of yourself—I mean, when you leave here you said you were going to go see Alvin Ailey dance company straight from the train station, Ms. Style Critic!

MICHELE: Yes, I'm going to that tonight.

MONTE: So write something about it, and from now on you're a style critic. Will you come back in six weeks and we can talk about how working your Quantum Affirmations affected you and your circumstances?

MICHELE: Yes, I will.

Michele: Six Weeks After Our Initial Session

MONTE: When last we met, we were talking about you being a style critic, about owning that as your overarching identity for a while, trying it on to see how it fit. Now, have there been any changes in your life on that front?

MICHELE: Oh yes, I mean, most definitely. I've actually been meeting a lot of artists and designers. I've gone back to an environment where I have the opportunity to meet a lot of people that are in the arts, too. Prior to that, I was not seeking that out, but lately I have been doing so and as a result of that I've been hanging out with producers and curators. I mean, just almost magically I meet these people and I don't know what they do, and then they tell me and I think, *Wow, very exciting*. I also have been approached to be a style writer for the *Examiner*.

MONTE: Well, there you go. You saved the best for last!

MICHELE: Yes, and it was actually kind of magical. I just got an e-mail and they said, "We would like for you to write about style for our New York Style section."

MONTE: Well, that's a miracle and it's your proof. By doing Quantum Affirmations we can have large miracles but we can also have a lot of small miracles that lead to the bigger miracles. Do you remember any changes in your attitude that you think might have led you to be more open to being approached that way or meeting with the exciting group of people you described?

MICHELE: I think when I was here last time I had a real breakthrough in terms of imagining myself in a different genre in terms of thinking what was possible, what was available to me. You know that before I worked with you last time I felt like I was not really connected to my passion, but then when I left here I felt a little bit more connected because I had identified something to envision in my quantumplaytion. That, in and of itself, was an accomplishment for me.

Before I couldn't identify where I was going or where I really wanted to go. So just being able to identify that actually brought it closer to me and brought it closer to the feeling that I wanted to experience and also the type of people that I wanted to meet. When I think back on it, it's amazing because, like I've said, I've just been immersed in a whole lot of very artistically rich cultural environments.

MONTE: You're giving me chills. Years ago in the subways, there was a poster with the image of a lot of big crayons on it and it affected me deeply. It was for New York's School of Visual Arts. That poster was done by a woman I would meet and become a close friend of later in my life, the world-renowned photorealistic artist Audrey Flack. The headline of that poster said, "The Times Call for Multiple Careers," and I took that to heart.

I think one of the problems that we all have here in the twenty-first century is that a lot of the goals and career goals and what we're going to do in our future haven't even been invented yet. How successful a person can become nowadays has a lot to do with multitasking and becoming multitalented and multifaceted, like you naturally are. We don't have enough examples of that to model for younger people coming up, though at the time of our conversation, actors Natalie Portman and James Franco are certainly two of them.

And you're joining their ranks. I'm proud of you for doing your Quantum Affirmations regularly, even though there was no guarantee that you'd have such dramatic results. And you're following in our footsteps and going beyond them, taking a metaphysical approach to your style criticism, which was another of your goals. You're setting a fine example for your daughter, and we have to share my Quantum Affirmations techniques with the younger generation.

Things are so different now. I think it is harder to be a young person now than it was for me. Everything is being written about and archived on the Internet; it's all there to see and explore. When I was growing up, I was never shown that I could be an inventor of metaphysical systems that teach intuition, Tarot, astrology, or affirmations. I remembered recently that my early Quantum Affirmations–powered quantumplaytions were about having sort of superpowers, like being psychic, but I don't think I really believed that it was possible for me. It's a good thing I let my imagination run with it.

When I was older I never consciously thought I could be a psychic or all these things that I ended up doing every day. My choices were limited, or so I thought. I could be a policeman like my father, I could be doctor, I could be these kinds of things, but I knew deep down that I could not because I didn't want to.

So, in your case, by doing the Quantum Affirmations quantumplaytion, you've planted your flag in this new kind of future with great results. We don't even know what it's going to be tomorrow, but here we are in that future you were just starting to visualize six weeks ago. Practicing Quantum Affirmations is like practicing using a time machine. When we do the visualizations, it is as if we're visitors from the future we want to get to and have come back to tell ourselves how to do it.

MICHELE: Oh yes, I definitely feel it. I feel like a pioneer moving forward, and the people that I'm meeting—they're also pioneers, and it's almost as if by magic we connect on a level that's very synchronistic. Everything that I've done is basically part of my quantum leap into my future, like it's prepared me for what I'm about to do right now, you know.

MONTE: Yes, and it's going to be just as magical from this time forward. When you did your Quantum Affirmations, did you do them in the morning, at night, or both? I would love to know what you did, how you did them, because, though I give people the basic information about how to do their quantumplaytion, I always hope that they are going to evolve their own way of how to do it and use their own way to see things, hear things, or however they're going to do it. So, if you could tell me how, did you see things when you did your quantumplaytions or did you hear things, or both?

MICHELE: Well, I did vision work, basically. I try to do it at night and in the morning, right before I go to bed as well as when I get up in the morning. Now it's second nature; I just have to have that feeling first thing. The first time, the vision part was tough—until I realized that of course it would be if I kept doing it without the feeling part. I'm a feeling-oriented person. So then I was not so focused on what kind of future events I wanted to experience. I focused on, *How do I want to feel?*

Focusing on how I wanted to feel in the future I was moving toward was key for me. I said to myself, *Okay, I want to feel accepted. I want to feel comfortable.* You know, I want to feel like everyone gets me. I want to feel understood. I don't want to feel like people are thinking, "Oh, she is weird!" I knew I wanted to feel like I'm okay, in a very comfortable position.

So I guess I actually expanded my energy throughout the day to magnetize things to me that were really important. I came to actually have that feeling of connecting my reality to my affirmation. That was important.

When I did my quantumplaytions I thought about all of the things that I really like. That made doing them really pleasant. I definitely recognize the power you get by pushing yourself past your limitations. There is a wall there. In my quantum-playtions I sometimes see a physical wall, and I see myself going over it and sometimes I smash through it.

It's like that in my life, too, when I am trying to do something and I have to push myself past that invisible wall of my own making. And that's when I'm having that feeling, you know, like there is that little voice that says, *Oh God, you're crazy, that's not going to happen, that's not going to work.* But now when I hear that I know that's the old tape playing. And then, because I'm in the Quantum Affirmations head, I think, *No, it will work. Calm down.* And then I have to really push past the negativity, almost like I'm pushing through a wall—a wall that I've created. Now I recognize that I've created this wall. When I'm doing my affirmations, my quantumplaytions, what helps, too, is pushing past that wall and saying, *Okay, no matter what this other voice is saying to me, I can feel differently about it*, and then, from there, making myself feel different.

Now I'm all about magnetizing myself with the entire QA technique, entangling my gift with my goal, doing my quantumplaytion, embracing the negative and the positive, like the poles on a magnet. I know that I am attracting my desires to me, almost like focusing on being like an energy source that's generating attractive magnetism. That's really what I've been trying to do, working that way with my affirmation versus just going back to feeling so lost and ungrounded. QA grounds you. Sure, you know it's challenging, but so is everything else, including not doing anything and letting life blow you around. It's not like it's something that you really have to focus and concentrate on. I just said it, but the truth is that you have to push yourself past yourself.

> *He who overcomes others is great.*
> *He who overcomes himself is greatest.*
> —Sun Tzu

MONTE: Right, what you're describing is what the Chinese general Sun Tzu said: "He who overcomes others is great. He who overcomes himself is greatest." He recognized that to be a good general or warrior, you have to get past the natural fear that's trying to keep you alive and keep you safe and keep you from being hurt.

MICHELE: Yes, and it's a day-to-day thing. Every day I have to do that.

MONTE: Oh, it's like brushing your teeth. You've got to do it twice a day, every day.

MICHELE: Yes, because if I stop, I feel that sense of *Oh, something's not right. Something's missing.*

MONTE: As a psychic who reads for a lot of very successful people, I know they feel exactly the same way as everybody else does, because every once in a while they will think, *Oh my God, I'm fooling everybody,* or *Oh my God, I can't do this,* and the reason they were successful was that they showed up. They do what they're going to do whether they are afraid or not, and they put it out there to be judged because what else can you do? You could just either sit back and complain about things or you could get out there and do it.

MICHELE: Exactly, and even now that I'm meeting all these people and artists, and I've met curators and so many people in art and culture, I still have this sense of, *Okay, what am I supposed to do with this information?*

MONTE: Well, the beauty is that you've evolved a way to take the information and do something with it by processing it as a style critic.

MICHELE: Another thing that I've actually thought about since I left here is artist management.

MONTE: Wow, we did talk about that. We touched on it. Michele: I think we sort of scanned this the first time, but that could actually be an even more probable future as well, because as I speak to the different artists, they tell me things. We talk about the way they're growing their career and they tell me that I have good ideas. Then on the Internet, I came across this whole manual on artist management.

MONTE: Management is an art. In a way, it's a separate area of the law. A lot of attorneys don't practice, but they practice as entertainment managers. I know several and they do quite well. This is a classic example of how what you want is an evolving process.

MICHELE: Yes.

MONTE: A lot of times people will think, *This is what I want and when I get there I'm going to do exactly this and nothing else.* But what happens is that your Quantum Affirmation brings you to the next stage of your process, and your goals evolve because you're in a different place than before and you have actually changed your beliefs, especially about what it is possible for you to achieve.

MICHELE: Exactly.

MONTE: Quantum Affirmations never bring you to the end of the line. The goalposts move as soon as you score your touchdown, as soon as you achieve your goal. You are obviously on quite the journey, where you can be doing more than one thing, achieving more than one goal. A lot of times people ask me as a psychic, "Should I do this or should I do that?" Quite often I hear that they should do both because the times really do call for multiple careers, much more today than back when I first saw that poster.

MICHELE: Yes, and also, with the artist management, it's a lot of reading and a lot of studying about a lot of things.

MONTE: A lot of handholding.

MICHELE: A lot of handholding, and the protocols and getting other people involved and networking, etcetera. So I thought about that, too, in terms of styling—you have to style them, you have to critique them, you have to write things for them, you are always looking through all these materials to actually promote, yet another thing about which we talked. Promoting artists and promoting things that I'm interested in is so important to me now. At first, I wanted to simply write about artists I saw. Then I liked a couple of them so much that I said to myself, *Maybe I should promote this; I could make money off this.*

MONTE: Certainly. There are a lot of people making money off of that, and right now...

MICHELE: Off of promoting people.

MONTE: Yes, it's a whole industry.

MICHELE: You know, so the style critic, yes, but the style promoter, the sales—because I'm in sales. It keeps evolving.

MONTE: Yes, as you are evolving as a person, it is logical that your goals and the scenes you create in your quantumplaytions are evolving, too.

MICHELE: I am a natural salesperson, so why not help sell the creativity of these people that I really like and make some money off of it. So I've been thinking that in that way, too, that one thing led to the other.

MONTE: Well, the good news is that you have supportive friends—not everyone does. When you come and tell us about all these different ideas, we're going to say, yes, go for it. Not everyone will, because they'll be scared to support such direct and honest and fearless action. Most people are scared to even hear about someone taking risks and getting out there to forge the life they want. This threatens the people who are allowing fear to stop them from doing the same.

A lot of times people are in a position where they'll tell their friends to slow down, don't risk trying something new. That's usually because these friends are not ready to put themselves out there and not ready themselves to acknowledge all the different aspects of their own potential career path. They will have a tendency to tell you, "Oh no, slow down. You should focus on the tried-and-true. Don't rock the boat." When I did my second book, *The Enchanted Tarot*, a publisher whom I love and I still work with told me, "Don't write about Tarot. You should just stay with astrology, the subject of your first book, *Karma Cards*, and concentrate on that." Well, I'm glad I didn't listen to him because *The Enchanted Tarot* sold hundreds of thousands of copies and is a classic, still in print since 1990.

MICHELE: Wow.

MONTE: When people give you that kind of advice, you have to say, "I respectfully decline to listen to you." You have to be strong enough to get past any obstacle, and sometimes the obstacle is going to be the people who love you the most, who are going to say no to you working to attain your deepest desire, because they don't want to see you get hurt.

MICHELE: Oh, yes.

MONTE: They will say, "Well, you should just concentrate on this one thing because this is making you money, so don't do that." You have to do what you want to do, not what other people want you to do.

MICHELE: Well, you know what I've learned? I just like doing the work, so I'm going to just keep knocking on the doors of my perception and the doors of the people I meet, and the doors that open, I'm going to go in.

MONTE: Right, because if you're not failing, you're not trying. Then, the next stage in your Quantum Affirmations is going to be dealing with success. That is something that scares a lot of people, too. There are a lot of people who are more comfortable thinking about, "When I get out of the situation I'm in and get to that point, wouldn't it be great?" and all of a sudden success has happened and they've put the past behind them, even though they haven't really adjusted to their new normal. It's a whole new world.

MICHELE: I'm so glad you've mentioned that, because that has been my next step. I've actually started affirming being financially secure and not worrying about having things work for me. That's what made me think about artist management, because I thought, *Wow, if I could book these people and make money off of them, that's a great way to make money.* I'm booking them, but they are doing the work, really. I'm helping them so they can do the work. I've thought, *If I could do that and have two clients, three clients, and then I can start booking them places, that's a great way to generate income based on using all my gifts.* Even my experience with fragrances comes into play, helping people use it to meditate, like I did with this woman I met recently.

MONTE: It sounds like you're right in the pocket with this, that you're accepting each new stage and you're starting to plan for the next stage of your Quantum Affirmation. No matter what particular job or career we are talking about, it is always a process of accessing one's abilities, strengths, and weaknesses. Growth is a sure sign that we are living.

MICHELE: I'm totally seeing the place I want to live one day soon. I'm even thinking about my daughter, visualizing her in situations. I am looking at my life and really quantum leaping, quantum jumping into the next thing. I like the way things are looking and feeling. I'm more content with the way things are.

I'm all right with here right now because I visit the future in my quantumplaytion, and when I do I think, *Yes! This is where I'm going!* So I don't feel trapped; I feel like I'm on a journey. I'm feeling how I want to be, where I want to live, and how I want to feel. I'm more aware of the things I want to do, and I don't worry that I won't get to do them. I have more confidence and a lot less doubt about myself and about the universe's ability to help me go where I want to go in the future. It even extends to how I want to look. Everything about me—I feel like it's shifting into a new lifestyle. So that feeling, that whole feeling of loving everything, mixed with the visualization really helped to change my energy.

MONTE: Well, I love having you here. Thank you so much, Michele.

MICHELE: Oh, you're welcome.

Michele: Twelve Weeks Later

MICHELE: After twelve weeks of applying Quantum Affirmations, my career path is getting clearer and clearer. A talent that I have not been using has suddenly come into play again. I have been a licensed makeup artist and skin-care specialist since 1984. Since the filming, I have done a photo shoot and a makeup lesson for a personal shopping client. Both of these women just asked me out of the blue, "Do you do makeup?" Both sessions reminded me of how talented I am with makeup and skin care. I have also been booked to do fashion and beauty consultations at a conference, as well as style a fashion show. Even though my path appeared to be about lifestyle and metaphysical writing and critiquing, my original query was about guidance and the congruency of my talents. The opportunities keep appearing, and I am consistently meeting people who are guiding me along the path. I have also realized a latent goal that keeps recurring and that is highlighting my artistic talents in the media through writing as well as TV. As I am writing this, there are a lot of opportunities in the works!

Joyce: A Letter from Italy

Here is a success story we received from Joyce, who used my Quantum Affirmations techniques:

JOYCE: I want to share with you my experiences of the past year. I celebrated my sixtieth birthday in April and my dreams came true when my family bought me the special Law of Attraction necklace designed by Amy…I was so excited to have it and wear it every day. Normally, I would never suggest a present for them to buy, but somehow, after going on the Enchanted World Web site and seeing that beautiful necklace, I knew there was something magical about it that spoke to me.

Becoming sixty is a sort of life marker, a time to reflect, to show gratitude for life thus far, and to streamline and formulate what it is one is here on earth for…With the economy being on the downside, it was hard to say that I must go to Italy again, and we knew we needed to rent the house out for the summer, and we did! It was a tremendous amount of work to stage the house, put things away, and then pack for Italy, but I was following my dreams by doing my Quantum Affirmations: seeing what I wanted, saying it, and feeling that it was real. And feeling the difficulty of it at the same time… that helped me to make it "real."

I put on the necklace and started my practice of visualizations and affirmations, using your tips, in April…the image on the talisman has an outstretched hand capturing a shooting star…this symbolizes for me that when we reach out, stretch our belief system, have faith, and go for our dreams, then anything is possible. By May I had an art exhibit at CW Post College and another one in June at Romany Kramoris Gallery in Sag Harbor. All of this required much work, and some money to get things prepared, but I did sell a few things in both places, and that spoke volumes to me about the economy—when you produce work that speaks to other people and they feel moved enough to buy it.

Spending three months in Tuscany, I walked up the mountains every morning, looking out over the hills of Chianti at the vineyards and olive groves and breathing in the fresh air...what a delight for my soul...what an enormous amount of space and energy...I sang and was joyous every day, every moment, and asked the universe for some recognition of my artwork...The creative juices were flowing, but I needed to exhibit my work and get it out there. I did my Quantum Affirmations, meditated on that mountaintop each day, and then returned to paint and paint for hours...Sure enough, due to the vibrational, quantum energy of your manifesting technique, not only was I offered one show for my work, but three!

My landlord came by every so often and was awestruck by my work. Then she brought a friend over who is an architect and works on archeological digs and restores some of the buildings in the medieval towns. She loved my work and promised to help me get my work exhibited. Following her visit, she called a curator from Turin, and he came down to look at my work. He was also impressed and wanted to select three paintings for a show that opened the following week!

I was not sure at first that I could get it together—that is part of the doubt, insecurity, and stumbling blocks that you describe in doing the Quantum Affirmations. But I believed I could do it anyway.

I followed my ritual of walking up the mountain, breathing in that fresh air and gazing over the countryside, and stroking my Law of Attraction talisman while seeing my dream as a movie in my mind's eye. I came back knowing that I had the strength and determination to make it all happen!

The first show was part of an international women's art exhibit in Casole d'Elsa. It was a wonderful experience, but I suffered a bit from wondering if my work would be up to par with everyone else's. There really was no reason to doubt. The next thing that happened was that the same curator loved my work so much, he needed an artist for a solo show but it had to be put up by the next week. He asked me if I could produce five more paintings. I was flabbergasted! I love to paint, but I do it on my own timetable, and now I had to perform under pressure. I rose to the occasion and was thankful for the opportunity to do what I love to do, and so I had the second one...a solo exhibit in Certaldo Alto, and then a third show of my paintings and photographs from a wonderful photographer who was inspired by my paintings...all in medieval towns in Tuscany...It does not get better than that! And they were well attended and a painting was sold!

Now I have been offered a fourth show in Venice opening on the twenty-first of June in a restaurant gallery in San Polo...

It is amazing to me how everything seems to flow when you follow your heart's desires and recite Quantum Affirmations both silently and out loud as a regular practice. My paintings are a mixture of what I see and what I feel, and the colors and the light in Tuscany and here on the East End are nothing short of the deepest inspiration! The symbolic beauty of the Law of Attraction necklace with the outstretched hand to the universe represents, for me, an elegant way of approaching life…Combining it with belief in yourself and your dreams really, really works!

Thanks, Amy and Monte, for your unique and creative take on life and showing people how to empower themselves!

Quantum Affirmations

CHAPTER 11

CASE STUDY
QUANTUM AFFIRMATION FOR WEALTH—DAVID

David: Before

MONTE: Let's talk about how to use Quantum Affirmations to improve one's financial situation. So many of people's problems usually boil down to an economic problem. So, David, the way Quantum Affirmations works is you try and get yourself to a probable future that you want rather than stumbling into a probable future that is the result of your not using your power to create your future more to your liking. I believe there's a science behind it, and the techniques of Quantum Affirmations seem to be at the very least symbolically related to some of the most basic and proven tenets of quantum physics, also known as quantum mechanics.

Scientific or not, I've found that I've discovered a system that works, that helps me get to the probable future I'd most like to see. I want to share that with you. The way we start off on this journey to the future is to try and figure out what your goal is. So what would your goal be?

DAVID: Well, my goal is to be a successful investor. I spend a lot of time investing money, and I haven't had any tragedies or anything, but I'm looking to invest in the right stocks.

MONTE: But are you talking about making a big score and then retiring, or do you enjoy the process of investing? Is the process of investing your passion? One of the things with Quantum Affirmations is to really charge up the energy of the quantum leap you're going to make. You try and go for a goal that you're passionate about. Most people are passionate about money. There's nothing wrong with that. In the Bible it says that the *love* of money is the root of all evil, not money in and of itself.

DAVID: I'm very, very, very passionate about the stock market.

MONTE: I know you have studied it in college and have a degree in finance.

DAVID: I like to trade in it all the time. But a lot of the time, there are things that I want to do with it, that I know I should do, but I won't get the courage to do it because of whatever mental block is stopping me, and I'll look back and say, *Ugh! I wish I had done that.*

MONTE: You mean you are angry with yourself for not getting past your natural resistance to investing a larger than normal amount because your intuition is telling you to? So the future you want to create has to be less fearful of backing up a hunch or an intuition. I don't blame you. Fear seems to short-circuit our nervous system and cause us to stop in our tracks when we should take action or it causes us to do things we later wish we hadn't done.

DAVID: Exactly. I'm too fearful. Even when I'm confident in the investment, I will still not take the risk, which is always necessary to take when you're investing. So instead of invest-ing the amount of money that I said to myself would be a good idea, would be a wise thing to do, and which another investor would probably say would be a wise thing to do, I'll invest only half of what I wanted to, out of fear.

Then the stock does well and I'll say to myself, *Ugh! I wish I had invested like I knew I should.* Sometimes I won't even act on an investment when I'm really superconfident. Right now, I'm going through that with gold and also with a Chinese stock called Dang, which is a really ridiculous word, but they're a Chinese Internet company that is modeled after Amazon.com.

MONTE: Interesting.

DAVID: And they are already established and profitable, and I'm very confident in the stock. But it takes a lot of energy to research a stock properly, and I waste a lot of time and energy not making the decision, procrastinating. I let my fear stop me from doing what I know is the right thing to do, and that makes me angry with myself. It's not a pleasant way to feel.

MONTE: When you say that you have fear...I believe fear is a natural reaction to the unknown. Fear exists in us to keep us as safe and secure as we can be in this world of change. Fear is all about self-protection. So let's examine your fear. What do you think you're afraid of? Are you afraid that you'll be wrong and be mad at yourself? Or are you afraid that you'll be wrong and someone else will say, "Oh, you were wrong"?

DAVID: Exactly.

MONTE: Or are you afraid that you'll go all-in and end up being broke, which is legitimate, of course, to be afraid of?

DAVID: Of course. I think the biggest fear is not so much what I'll lose, because I always set up my investments so I'll know what the maximum amount is that I'll lose.

MONTE: It sounds like you're a cautious investor.

DAVID: But I definitely set restrictions—*Oh if this doesn't work, what will so-and-so think of this? What would my dad think if I lose this money or if this doesn't play out as a smart thing to do?* But what ultimately ends up happening—when I have those thoughts—is I waste the time where I should have made the investment. Then as time goes on, I haven't made the wise decision; I made the incorrect decision.

MONTE: Right. As a counselor, most of my work is actually done with corporations, determining who to keep, who to fire, when they merged, back in the merger days. Now it's who to keep, who to fire, as corporations shed people. But I work with a lot of very wealthy people, a lot of investors, and they all have the same issue that you're talking about. They all think, *I should've done this,* and they worry about the one that got away. When you find yourself worrying about being judged by a particular person—you mentioned your father—what would happen if he made a similar decision and screwed up or lost it all or had the same reaction? How would you judge him? Because usually the reason that you wouldn't want to be judged by him is because you might judge him that way if he lost, if he made the same kind of bet.

So then we get into the realm of forgiveness and also decoupling. When you do Quantum Affirmations, you want to quantum entangle yourself with the future that you want. It sounds like you might be quantum entangled with the situation that you want to decouple from so you can move off on your own. This sounds like it's a differentiation type of issue, in terms of the fear of the judgment from your father, but it's totally legitimate; to me it sounds like you're just playing it cautious.

This is the strange thing: If someone came to you with the same thing you're coming to me with, you'd probably say, "Well, it's no big deal." This is true of everybody's problems, including my own. One of the interesting things is that it's not so much that there's anything wrong with us, but that we *think* there's something wrong with us. Let's say I came to you and I said, "I have this great idea to invest in this stock, but I just can't do it; I can't bring myself to do it." You've studied investment. You've gone to college for it; you have a degree in it. What would you tell me?

DAVID: I would say that you've really got to get over that because it's important to invest. It's very easy to say that, but...

MONTE: Let's say I'm investing but I just can't bring myself to go all-in when I have these hunches. Because you're talking about hunches, now you're in my realm, the psychic stuff.

DAVID: I would never go all-in on something. I guess I'm having a fear of investing in things that I really would like to be investing in—but I have a fear of what's going to happen if I'm wrong. I think I'd like an affirmation that will prevent me from doing that. Because it prevents me, I would say, 20 percent to 30 percent of the time before I buy a stock. There have been maybe three out of ten times I buy a stock that I really want to buy, and I've done my research, and I've really, really, really thought about it. I'll get ready to make the investment, and then three out of ten times—I'm just throwing a number out there—but 30 percent of the time I'll say, *No, maybe I shouldn't.*

MONTE: But have there been times when you're glad you didn't do it? When you thought it was going to go up and if you hadn't gone in...

DAVID: Not usually. Usually the investments that I want to do are the ones that I think are...

MONTE: But do they actually end up working in the future?

DAVID: Yes, when you do the research.

MONTE: Well then, you've definitely got to do it.

DAVID: Yes, so I mean…

MONTE: It's not like you're just some guy off the street. You're trained in this. So what you're saying is, "I'm trained in something, I'm not using my training the way I could be, and I'm missing out on certain stocks."

DAVID: I want to get past that mental block that happens to me three out of ten times at trade.

MONTE: Gotcha! Well, three out of ten is actually not that bad. Seventy percent of the time you're doing pretty well. Your Quantum Affirmation situation is also interesting in the sense that it's not really a different kind of future that you're looking to create. You're looking to just tweak the present.

DAVID: Yes, well, the future that I want is financial growth.

MONTE: It sounds like you've got to stop caring what other people are thinking, and in a way you've got to stop caring what you think.

DAVID: Yes, that's actually a very interesting point.

MONTE: You know, because you're second-guessing yourself.

DAVID: Yes.

MONTE: So as a psychic, you stop second-guessing yourself when you've been right enough. And if you're right seven out of ten times, you can make a living. I mean, Las Vegas exists because they're right six out of ten times.

DAVID: You're right, sure. Well, I guess as we're talking, what I'm starting to realize is that what I'd really like is an affirmation that will help me from freezing on decisions that I know both intuitively and logically are decisions that I want to make.

MONTE: Okay. Well, with Quantum Affirmations what we're trying to do is to entrain and entangle yourself with the future that you want. You try and feel as positive about that future, that new goal that you have, as you are about something that you already have a gift for, something that flows to you effortlessly and endlessly, something that you feel like you have enough of and you can do really easily.

Now, that could be something that you do in sports. I know you used to row. It could be something like that. If you can be really good at one thing, you can be really good at another thing. So if you are to examine your life and what flows endlessly and effortlessly for you…maybe you're great socially or writing—something where you never think to yourself, *Oh, I'm going to freeze* or *I don't have enough of it.*

DAVID: Well, I would say writing. I always feel that I can do that effortlessly. And conversing I think I can do effortlessly, too.

MONTE: For sure.

DAVID: Probably those two are the main things.

MONTE: Okay, something where you never think, *I'll be at a loss for words* or *I'll say the wrong thing.*

DAVID: Yes.

MONTE: Because what you're saying is, "I'll bet on the wrong thing."

DAVID: Right.

MONTE: What you want to do is transfer that same feeling to this future self that you're going to be. The main problem with affirmations is not that we don't know how to do them, but that we know how to do them too well. The affirmations that we do too well are "I don't have enough money to do this" or "If this happens, this will happen," and you're affirming it, and so you're creating that future. You've got to create a different future.

The basic affirmation you want to do is to see yourself in the future. You close your eyes and see yourself in your mind's eye as looking at the stock market and seeing that a trade that you've made has come through really well. One of the downsides of a trade you make going through really well is that here comes some unforeseen consequence you didn't expect to happen. If you thought you had made all this money, would having a lot of money be a problem? Would being that accurate then force you into having to be that accurate every time? Is it a perfectionist thing?

With Quantum Affirmations, we see the goal that we want, but we see it as realistically as we can. We step outside of ourselves and then step into ourselves in the new reality, and so you see the good things that are going to come with it. But there has to be bad, because when you make a bright light, there are always shadows, and the bright light of the future is you making these trades and not being anxious about them. You know, you've gotten rid of that, but out comes the new issue. So can you see any new issues that would come up if you didn't have the issue of second-guessing yourself and not doing the trade?

DAVID: Probably having the ability to keep it going . . .

MONTE: That's logical.

DAVID: Running into the fear of *Okay, well, now that it's good, I don't want to lose it.* I've actually struggled with that on other things, things that I'd done well on, then maybe sold out of. But it's hard for me to say, "What do I use this money for now?" So that's a fear of not being sure where the next thing is. But the real issue is being able to make the decision when really everything is telling me I should make the decision. But there really has been more than one occasion when I won't make the decision.

MONTE: I know you talked about being the most confident before, when you had done the research.

DAVID: Yes.

MONTE: As somebody who does psychic readings, there are times when I don't know what I'm talking about at a certain level when I'm doing a psychic reading. Like when I told someone to buy CSX, I didn't know what CSX was. But it ended up being the right thing for this person to buy. Or when I said to someone, "Buy Apple at eighty-five dollars," and now it's over three hundred dollars. I knew I had an Apple computer but I didn't know anything about the stocks. So is it that you don't want to trust your intuition?

DAVID: Maybe it's a lack of trust in myself.

MONTE: Well, most people are not raised to trust their intuition; most people discount intuition as part of the equation because they forget that kings and the rich and powerful have consulted psychics and Tarot readers and astrologers since time began. Is it an issue with not wanting to think, *It's only my intuition*? But every successful investor says, "I had the feeling," or "I had it in my gut," or "I fly by the seat of my pants." So is that the issue? It sounds like you're ready to make a breakthrough and trust your own intuition more, just because it's coming from you.

DAVID: Yes, well, I've always tried to train myself to think that if I have a gut feeling, that will not ever be the reason why I buy.

MONTE: And it shouldn't be the main reason.

DAVID: Right.

MONTE: But it's part of the process.

DAVID: Right. That's an interesting point. You have to allow that intuition to not paralyze you. I'll get to the point where I'm ready to buy or sell, and then I'll get to that intuition point and wonder, *Is this the right thing to do?* Even if my intuition says yes, I still sometimes won't make the decision to do it.

MONTE: Now that we've established that intuition is part of the mix, we have to put it at an appropriate level. I think we should formulate a Quantum Affirmation–powered quantum-playtion that can bring your gift to your goal, the goal being feeling more confident to pull the trigger on an investment that you've done the research on and that you've been led to by your intuition. You've done your research. Now you're in a position where you have to pull the trigger and actually spend the money and do it. So now we have to balance out where your intuition is in the situation.

DAVID: Shall I close my eyes?

MONTE: Yes, please, and then see yourself in your mind's eye doing what it is that you do that flows endlessly and effort-lessly, which is writing. I think in your case, you're going to have to write or speak to yourself, see yourself as your future self, and tell yourself in the way you would write that, just as easy as writing is for you, that's how easy investing is for you; that's how easy getting into this future position where you're a successful investor who knows that you're going to be wrong sometimes but you're going to be right more; that there's no reason to be afraid, because you're never going to be out on the street.

You write this down and see, instead of ink coming out of your pen, money's coming out of your pen. Money's coming out of your mouth and it's just forming beautiful piles on the table. Because in the future, you'll be able to say these things and feel good about them rather than having your intuitions about stocks be a problem for you. Right now, even the ones that work as much as they work for you—it's like they're being dragged out of you. They're being dragged out of you, and it's causing you pain.

So in the future, the positive aspect of it is that this money is going to flow. The negative aspect is that you're going to have to do it again. And then the positive aspect is that you *can* do it again because you've done it before. And if you make a mistake, so what? You can handle it. You don't bet more than you can afford. All investing is gambling, after all.

And if there's a concern that your investments in companies, situations, or world politics are negative and might hurt people, well, there's hardly anyone alive who isn't doing something that isn't good for the planet. At this point, you can continue to invest in them and then use excess money that you have to contribute to remedial charities or things that you can do to help and possibly get into a political situation that would help.

So you see yourself as something other than just making money. The future you is writing, using this gift to write this endless money, write yourself these checks that are going to help people and maybe even get into a political future to help people, and it's something that makes your heart open rather than close. Now open your eyes. What were you feeling? What were you seeing? How was what I was saying making you feel?

DAVID: Well, it was very relaxing and made me feel like I could let go of the anxiety that I feel right before I make any kind of investment. Especially connecting in the writing; that was really interesting because connecting something that's so easy, that I almost don't think about, made me feel like it would be helpful. If I applied that thinking toward the anxiety I feel that stops me from making an investment when I'd found something that I actually know that I want to do, that would actually be pretty helpful. It was interesting.

MONTE: Yes, you don't want to say to your intuition, which has led you to this situation in the first place, "Give me a reason to *not* do this," which is basically what you're saying. As a psychic, I know that throws your intuition into spasms; that's not what I do. What I do is give you the stuff where you *don't* think about it. I'm going to lead you to places. I'm going to give you pictures and feelings and all the other stuff that allows you to accept your intuition. You're actually asking me to do the work that's for you to do.

DAVID: When I write, it's something I don't think about; I'm completely confident and relaxed when I do it. I'm confident that what I'm writing is good and it doesn't stop me from writing.

MONTE: Right.

DAVID: And when I do investments, I have the confidence that what I'm doing is good, but there's the fear of loss, I guess.

MONTE: You mean a fear of making a wrong bet and losing money?

DAVID: Yes, but it's not a real fear in a lot of ways because I've really, really done the research on the stock.

MONTE: Exactly. At a certain point, you can't blame yourself.

DAVID: Just like it wouldn't be a real fear to say what I'm writing is bad, because it's not a real fear. But a lot of the time that can happen with writing.

MONTE: Oh, yes.

DAVID: I could be thinking, *What if someone reads this?*

MONTE: Well, exactly . . .

DAVID: But that doesn't prevent me, so using that logic of applying the confidence I have in the writing to the confidence I have in researching the stock market, why would I have a fear of the outcome? In writing, you have an outcome that maybe people will like. With the stock market, the outcome might be that you'll lose a little bit.

MONTE: Well, you're asking yourself for certainty, and there's no such thing.

DAVID: Yes.

MONTE: Would you be willing to come back in a few weeks to see how things have gone? Whether it's easier for you to make the trades and how you feel about them, whether you're able to apply this new technique of visualizing at the same time of applying your gift to your goal?

DAVID: Sure, yes. That was actually really helpful, yes.

MONTE: Cool.

DAVID: I never thought about it that way.

David: Six Weeks After Our Initial Session

MONTE: How has the Quantum Affirmations technique affected your life, if it has?

DAVID: Well, I was really skeptical at first.

MONTE: It's good to be skeptical.

DAVID: But when you started explaining about visualizing doing something really easy and then applying that to something that you find challenging, I really thought that was an interesting way of thinking about things. So there's been this stock I've been eyeing for a long time. It's a Chinese ADR, which means you can buy into a foreign stock but through America.

MONTE: What does ADR stands for?

DAVID: American Depository Receipt.

MONTE: Gosh!

DAVID: So it's basically like buying a stock.

MONTE: I understand.

DAVID: But in another country. I've been following it forever. I felt really confident about it, but I was just nervous
like I always get when I'm investing because of fear of losing
money or failure or what other people would think if I lost.
But anyway, when I went to buy it, I really did sit there for a
minute and close my eyes and visualize myself writing, which
is something that comes really easily to me, and I bought it. I
bought it at a time that I wanted to buy it and didn't hesitate.

MONTE: That's great!

DAVID: Of course, during the next couple of weeks it went
down. It was even more interesting because I'm almost glad
that the stock went down for the next couple of weeks.

MONTE: It went down.

DAVID: It went down, and normally when that happens, my
reaction is to sell it, which is the stupidest thing you can do
when it comes to investing, but it's a very natural reaction.
When you watch a stock go down, you want to get rid of it.

MONTE: You want to cut your loss.

DAVID: Yes.

MONTE: So you don't lose the whole thing.

DAVID: I always set a limit, but it wasn't going down to the limit where I said, "Okay, this was a bad investment." When I had that instinct, which was wrong, to sell, especially during the second week, it was down almost 15 percent, and I had invested a significant amount of money. I was really confident in the stock, and I still am. I still own it. I just visualized to myself that, *Okay, I need to buy more of this while it's going down, because what's going on is that profit taking has happened because it's an IPO.*

MONTE: An initial public offering.

DAVID: Yes, and the reason it's going down is because people are taking their profits off of the IPO.

MONTE: So when the stock first is issued . . .

DAVID: It usually zooms, and then it comes down a little bit because people will get rid of it.

MONTE: Right, like Google was twenty-something dollars when it first came out and now its six hundred dollars.

DAVID: Right.

MONTE: But when it first came out, it did go down because people took the profit.

DAVID: It went up and then it goes down and then it goes up again.

MONTE: Then it gets real.

DAVID: Right. I knew that that's where I was, but it's so hard to understand that when you're in it.

MONTE: Because it's your money.

DAVID: Yes. So I did the same thing. I just said, *Just keep it.* It's as easy as writing, and *Buy more,* and it went up significantly from the 15 percent bottom that it had gone down.

MONTE: Did you buy more at the 15 percent off price?

DAVID: Yes, I bought more.

MONTE: At the bottom?

DAVID: Well, not at the total bottom but at a price much lower than what I initially paid for the stock.

MONTE: But still, that's good, because it's hard to time a total bottom.

DAVID: Yes, of course. Then it went back up to right around the price at which I bought it. So I'm ahead now. I'm still really very confident just based on the research and the business's company, which is essentially the Chinese Amazon, which is just an incredible business.

MONTE: Right. There's another stock that came out low and now is very big.

DAVID: Yes, and they have a dominant market share and the whole thing. It's crystal clear to me that I should be investing in this. I'm hanging on to it really comfortably. I feel at ease owning it, whereas normally, if I hadn't spoken to you, I'd feel a sense of anxiety. Especially when it was down, I would have felt a fear of what other people would think while it was down. I just kept visualizing that I was making it as easy as writing.

MONTE: And that helps you to calm down, because what you're describing to me is that you're doing what my clients who are successful investors do, which is when something goes down and they really believe in it, they buy more, an action that is counterintuitive.

DAVID: That's so hard to do, yes.

MONTE: It's like saying when you're falling, try and fall faster, but that is the way successful investors make money, and it also averages out the loss.

DAVID: Right now, I'm significantly up, but I really think that longer term it's going to be even more so, and I've always been confident about that from the beginning. But it's watching those fluctuations—that is where I get tripped up.

MONTE: Well, it seems that you understand the math and the logic and the nonemotional aspects of it, and what was tripping you up before, from what I recall from our last time, six weeks ago, was that you would get nervous and think that someone was going to judge you or you were going to judge yourself, and you weren't comfortable with the fact that you might have made investments that didn't work out in the past. You don't want to have that happening, which is all natural. Because who wants to lose money?

DAVID: Yes, of course, but it's interesting that you say that, because I've been applying the whole technique to a lot of other things, especially if I feel a sense of anxiety when I walk into a room. I'll do the same thing. I'll just visualize doing something easy, and visualizing will make that feeling of anxiety go away by feeling that emotion that feels easy. I was really surprised. I really appreciate it.

MONTE: Well, it's my pleasure. The reason I wrote the book and the reason we're doing this DVD is because it works for me.

DAVID: Of course, it makes sense.

MONTE: But when you realize something works, you want to share it with people, but you have to figure out how to share it with them, especially when people aren't ready. So you can do a book, which is wonderful, because when people are ready for it, they're going to buy the book. So that's how that group self-selects to be ready for it. But I don't blame anyone for being skeptical about it. Because from the sound of it, it just sounds like a bunch of New Age psychobabble, yet there are the quantum physics principles, which I intuitively believe to be underlying it, which is more comfortable for a numbers person. I'm one myself.

DAVID: Yes, it definitely worked for me.

MONTE: Great! We're talking about the concept of probable futures, and here we are. What I love about the DVD process is that here we are in the future from when we did our last session. Changes have happened and you've put yourself into the future that you want to be in, which was to be less anxious about investing. But as you say, it does spill over into other areas of life. When you did your Quantum Affirmation, how did you do it? Did you do it in the morning and at night? Or did you do it just at night? And what did you see and feel?

DAVID: I would know I was going to do an activity that was going to make me anxious or fearful, and I would just do it right before. It was effortless. I would just do it for three to ten minutes.

MONTE: Even during the day.

DAVID: Right while I was at the computer and about to make the trade. When I would normally be saying, *Am I going to do this? Am I going to hesitate?* I know I shouldn't, but I always very often do anyway.

MONTE: For me, anyway, one of the best things about Quantum Affirmations is that it makes you more aware of when you're doing the kinds of activities or the thing that's holding you back; you become aware of it.

DAVID: Yes.

MONTE: There's a philosopher, *Gurdjieff*, who said, "When falling asleep wakes you up, you know you're making progress." So you'd be anxious, and all of the sudden say, *Well, it's time to do the Quantum Affirmation because I'll probably be anxious.*

DAVID: Yes.

MONTE: So that's what's going on in your life. It really makes me feel good to hear you say all this.

DAVID: It makes me feel good that it worked.

David: Twelve Weeks Later

DAVID: At my twelve-week mark, Dang reported sensational earnings for the fourth quarter, and I've now made more than 10 percent on the stock and expect to make more. I've also invested in gold and in Amazon effortlessly, both of which are doing very well. Using your Quantum Affirmations technique of visualizing something that I do naturally into something I find challenging produces extremely clear thinking that's helped me tremendously.

CHAPTER 12

CASE STUDY
QUANTUM AFFIRMATION
FOR LOVE—MEG

Meg: Before

MONTE: Hi, Meg. The process that we're going to work on today is called Quantum Affirmations. Quantum Affirmations is a fivefold process. In the first part, we identify what your goal is. In the second part, we take your history with that goal and help you to work on whether that goal is really the issue that we're trying to get to in the Quantum Affirmations. Quantum Affirmations is all about transforming the future and using what is traditionally known as affirmations but also being aware of the scientific underpinning of affirmations, which is quantum physics, strangely enough. And even though quantum physics is all about atomic particles, I think that the micro cause does apply to the macro cause. And I think one day the quantum physicists will come to that conclusion, because if we listen to quantum physicists now, they sound like New Age shamans.

Now we're up to the third step, which is to identify your gift. Your gift is something that flows to you endlessly and effortlessly. And what you're going to try to do is entangle what flows to you endlessly and effortlessly, your gift, that which you don't even think about. There's a quantum concept called *quantum entanglement*. You're going to try to entangle your gift with your goal.

It bears repeating that in Tarot, there's a position of the Celtic Cross reading called "the hope or the fear." I was wondering why it's called that; then one day I realized that what you hope for is something that you don't have, and the reason you don't have it yet, unlike all the things you have, is that you're afraid of it. So once the fear element is—not necessarily gone, because fear is a natural self-protective mechanism. Once the fear element is part of the process, then you can move on and add that to your gifts, because that will start to flow endlessly and effortlessly.

The next stage is to get into the shadow aspect of what happens in the future, because I feel, without doubt, that this future is coming. And as we do the process, you might feel that way, too. And so, because bright lights make shadows, you're going to have those bright lights in your new future, and with that future are going to come the natural problems that arise. Inside your subconscious, which is so powerful, you can transform all kinds of things about you, and maybe even things about the future, because if you transform yourself, you transform the future.

The Quantum Affirmations are unlike traditional affirmations in that when you start doing them, you start seeing all the negatives that can arise; for example, if you win the lottery, the relatives will come out of the woodwork, you know. There's no way that's not going to happen. Even people who are not your relatives are going to come out of the woodwork asking you for money.

MEG: Right.

MONTE: So, at that stage of the entanglement with you in the future, you tell your subconscious mind that you're ready to deal with it. You tell it, "I've seen these negatives. I've seen some of them," because there's always the element of surprise. "I've seen these negatives that I can deal with." And then, after that, it is a question of doing it maybe once in the morning and before you go to sleep—when you wake up and go to sleep. It's not something that you have to do all the time.

MEG: Right.

MONTE: It also involves a process of visualization that is done traditionally with the eyes closed. Then there's what I call the Quantum Affirmations quantumplaytion, where you're visualizing, which is to imagine what's really going on, sort of like acting. So you tell me you're a Leo, so that will be easy. I'm a Leo rising, and the joke with Leo rising is this: Our stage fright is that we get scared when we're not on stage.

MEG: Okay.

MONTE: In acupuncture, they have what's called the presenting complaint, which is what brings you to the acupuncturist that day. What would you like to work on today with Quantum Affirmations? It can be anything, you know. We'll get down to what it really is, but we'll start off with what you think it is.

MEG: Well, at thirty-nine, there's a real big window of expiration here in terms of having a family.

MONTE: Coming forward.

MEG: Exactly. And a single parent is not something that I wanted naturally. I didn't want to go down that road.

MONTE: Okay. In Quantum Affirmations, the first question you ask once you've identified your goal is, Why do I want that? So that's the next question. Do you want to have a family because you really love children? Do you want a family because you think it's what you should do? What do you think is the reason why you think you have to do this—because you don't have to do anything.

MEG: Well, I've always wanted children.

MONTE: Okay.

MEG: I have. But it's been a bit of a conscious decision not to do it until...

MONTE: You're ready.

MEG: I thought I was ready. I've lived my life in a lot of regards. I've experienced things that I really wanted to experience. And that was an important part for me.

MONTE: So you're ready.

MEG: So I'm ready. Yes.

MONTE: Well, this sounds good. So are the children the important part, or is the soulmate the important part?

MEG: Well, I see you say that because I can certainly go and have children by myself . . .

MONTE: Yes. People do that a lot.

MEG: That would be plan B, so to speak.

MONTE: Right.

MEG: But the experience of being with someone you love and having children with somebody is what I want. Obviously, there are practical things involved...

MONTE: Sure.

MEG: You know, how you take care of those kids and having the means to do that.

MONTE: Well, I also think it's good for kids growing up to know men and women.

MEG: Right.

MONTE: And so you would be more comfortable doing the traditional marriage? Or you would be okay with living with this person?

MEG: No, marriage…I think that that's a crucial life experience to make those promises to somebody and enjoy raising these children together.

MONTE: I think it's great. As a counselor, I know that it's all about what the person wants. It's not what I think is right.

MEG: Right.

MONTE: I've been married since 1978. So that's a long time. I personally think marriage is a wonderful thing. But I would never presume when I'm working with someone with Quantum Affirmations to think that I can apply my values to you. So it sounds like you've thought about this. It sounds like you've worked on this.

MEG: Right.

MONTE: Okay. So we're in a good place that you know that this is really what you want. You want the soulmate and you want the children to grow up with you having your soulmate.

MEG: Correct.

MONTE: That's very ideal, but it's not unattainable. That's the first thing to realize. It's not unattainable, because people do it.

MEG: Right.

MONTE: So now we've identified your goal. What's your history with the goal? I can do this psychically and figure out what you've gone through, but I don't think that's what's going on here. And the reason I mentioned psychic ability is because it's going to come into play later, because everybody has it.

And that's really what we're doing with Quantum Affirmations. We're opening up people to their ability to create the future, which sounds magical and miraculous. But Einstein said, "There's two ways to live your life. Either like nothing is a miracle or like everything is a miracle." And I have a feeling he lived his life like everything is a miracle. And that's how I'm trying to live my life, and that's what Quantum Affirmations is all about, because you can change the future. Right now, we're changing the future by the decisions that we make. It's as if we are in a sci-fi movie and we've come back to this moment from the future you want to experience to set you on the right path to creating it.

So, how has your experience been with the quest? Because that's really what it is; it's mythical. Your mythical quest to find your soulmate—how has that happened in the past? What's happened? What's prevented it from happening, in your opinion?

MEG: Well, I was married when I was much younger. When I was very young—at twenty.

MONTE: That's young.

MEG: Yes. I was young. I think it would be the answer to everything at that point. I was twenty. And then after that, I really traveled for fifteen years.

MONTE: Wow.

MEG: Nonstop on the show circuit.

MONTE: So that's hard to have a relationship...

MEG: It's impossible.

MONTE: Unless you're with someone else who's also on the same tour.

MEG: Precisely, precisely. So...

MONTE: It's the like the circus, traveling constantly from one place to another, moving on just as you're getting settled.

MEG: Yes. So we, my animals and me, moved to East Hampton four years ago, and to get yourself off of that circuit is actually a really hard process, because your life—

MONTE: It's addictive.

MEG: First of all, I put a lot of thought behind where I wanted to make my roots and where I really wanted to establish a life. I tried a few places in East Hampton. It was the one that resonated with me the most, and I don't regret that decision. I love East Hampton. And then, really, it's been structured around growing my business.

MONTE: And your business is…? If you don't mind me asking.

MEG: I'm a horse trainer.

MONTE: Cool.

MEG: Yes. So it's really been nothing having to do with finding a soulmate and all about growing my business, which is an essential part of my being—what you have to offer to a relationship, right?

MONTE: Right.

MEG: And in many respects that's where my self-esteem is based.

MONTE: Well, it sounds like you don't want to make another mistake—because you said you were married young—because everything that you're telling me is right. The first rule of warfare is make your base secure. That's what you're doing. You were traveling, so you realize that a relationship when you're in that situation, unless it's with someone who is committed to the same travel plans—it's not going to work. And now you've made your base secure. You know where you want to be, and now you're at this point. And obviously, you're a good manifester, because you manifested this session with us in a very miraculous way. It's like we sent out a call to the universe and you came. So obviously, it's the right time. You have, apparently, a couple of gifts. One is that you're a really a good planner, and obviously your horse-training ability, which is kind of miraculous in itself because it has so lent itself to your Quantum Affirmations visualization. Because it sounds to me like when you go into a ring with the horse, you're not worried, "Will I know what to do with the horse? Will I know what this horse needs? Will I know what this horse is trying to tell me?" When you go in there, that's what you do, right?

MEG: That's what I do, and you know if you make a few mistakes, there's nothing that you can't undo to deal with those mistakes.

MONTE: Right. You know, in your case, in terms of your relationship, it doesn't sound like you've really been blocking yourself; it sounds like you've been waiting.

MEG: Yes. I think that that's really a fair thing to say.

MONTE: Yes. And so I don't know if we're really undoing blocks about it. As much as you're approaching the logical aspect of when to actually make the move to find someone, I bet that's why the Quantum Affirmations are going to work pretty quickly for you.

MEG: I think so. But at first, to be really honest, there is just one block I think that is a subconscious thing. I think the number one thing is that I gained more weight. And I think that in some subconscious way, that is...

MONTE: You're trying to push people away.

MEG: Yes. It's not an attractive thing. It's not going to attract the type of person that I would like to attract.

MONTE: But is the weight gain from a medical reason, or is it because you're more sedentary because you're not traveling? And you can actually eat instead of, "Hey, we've got to go."

MEG: I think it's probably a combination. I think it's probably a lot of factors. It's probably not just one or two. It's probably all of that.

MONTE: So, mentally and logically, you think it's time. But obviously there's some part of you that makes sense of, "No. I'm going to gain weight. And that's going to push away the person that I want to attract." But as a happily married man, I know that the person that you want to attract doesn't care if you gained weight or lost weight. The person that's right for you, the person that is going to be right for your particular life, loves you the way you are.

MEG: Right.

MONTE: So that's the first thing to remember—you can't fool him. You can't really push him away. But the other thing is that you're honest enough to know that. So let's apply the gift to a Quantum Affirmation that addresses both the issues. And yours is so easy because you're a trainer of horses. So you have to see this guy and this future as a situation in which you'll be training this guy. And there's nothing wrong with it—I'm not saying that you're going to take someone and they're going to be in the harness and you have the whip. I'm just saying that when you're in love with someone, you want to be there for them in any way you can.

MEG: Right.

MONTE: And there's the element of training with that. I know I do this with my wife. When I'm asking her a question, I want to know. I want to grow. So you're looking for someone to grow with. Okay, we'll do this with our eyes closed now. This is how a visualization works. Shakespeare had a beautiful way of putting it. He said, "You see in your mind's eye, a scene," and you don't have to think of it as being real or not real. Just see it for now.

And in your mind's eye, see what flows to you effortlessly and endlessly, which is at this point—I mean, it sounds like you've got a lot of gifts but this—well, let's work on the horse trainer because it's so perfect.

So here's the horse, and you're working with this horse in a place that you really like, a place where you feel comfortable, a place where you don't feel like, "Oh my God. I've got to pack up and go because the circuit is moving to another town." You're established; you're in East Hampton. Maybe you're even in a place that you've seen before.

You're totally comfortable. You're working with a horse you're comfortable with. And on that horse is this guy. This guy who is looking at you and is interested in you and doesn't care about anything except you because he likes the way you trained the horse. He likes your ability to train the horse without fear. The horse likes you, obviously.

And then the guy gets off the horse, and he's been nice to the horse, and to you. And then he hugs you, and it's obvious that there's attraction between the two of you. And you both hug the horse, and then you walk back to your house, and this is where you live; this is this person in the future that you've met.

And there are children there because this is part of the Quantum Affirmations. So you see the children and they're really happy because they love the horse and they love you. And they love all the animals that you have, and that's another gift you have, that you're really good with animals.

And this is a future that is real. There are an infinite number of possible futures, and this is one of them. This is the one that we're now quantum entangling with your present moment. The Law of Synchronicity states that "things done at the same time have a relationship that's significant." So now you've planted your quantum flag in this future; this is what you're telling your subconscious is the future that you want.

Now you can open your eyes. So we've matched the two things together with what you're really, really good at that flows totally easily and establishing this family relationship with someone who's a soulmate.

Now that we've done the affirmation where you've seen this guy riding the horse and you've walked back to the house where the kids are, how did that whole affirmation make you feel?

MEG: It felt natural, I guess, in a lot of ways, right?

MONTE: Well, it's what you're going for. Sure. So it seemed real?

MEG: It seemed real. That's what I'm telling you. Yes.

MONTE: That's good. Did you have any kind of fears associated with it? Any kind of joys associated with it? Did you see any particular aspects of the way anyone looked, because that could be really telling.

MEG: Really?

MONTE: Yes, because when you do stuff like that, it lets your psychic ability go, and you might even see the person; at the very least, you'll see the horse.

And you might see the kids and things like that.

MEG: I remember I looked happy and content. There's a sense of contentment about it.

MONTE: Well, that's powerful.

MEG: Security. Yes.

MONTE: Because women especially need to feel secure and protected.

And so you're identifying with this guy, that he's not crazy and is going to stay and want to be there and is the father of these children. So that was a good feeling?

MEG: It was peaceful. I was actually peaceful in a lot of ways.

MONTE: Good. The great thing is that the science underlying it says that if you do this and entangle everything together with your present moment, it will help your subconscious guide you to that future. Mixing psychology, the power of positive affirmations, and quantum physics is really what Quantum Affirmations is all about.

You don't really have the resistance to it so much. You just don't want to make a mistake. And that same thing can happen with a guy, because the reality of the situation is, you go and meet people. Sometimes it works; sometimes it doesn't. But to know that this future is really possible and can flow as easily and effortlessly and endlessly as your abilities that do flow like that. You've just got to keep them together.

So every time you slip into eating more than you think you should or thinking it can't happen, which I haven't heard you say, so you probably know that it can happen. You just do this Quantum Affirmation, and it's not putting you into a fantasy world. That's the interesting thing. I have a great relationship, and the whole Quantum Affirmations program grew out of the fact that I didn't understand, "Why me? Why me? I mean, I'm a jerk like every other guy in the world. How? Why?"

And then it's just like when we were asked to write a book about relationships called *The Soulmate Path*. These people said, "Now you can write a book. We've just bought this publishing company. You can write a book about your relationship secrets." I said, "We don't have any secrets." They said, "Well, you better get some secrets because we're going to publish this book."

So when I sat down, I realized, "Wow. We *do* do things. We put the relationship first." That's what I realized: "Oh my God. We really do, don't we?" And it's just like what you do when you're working with your animals or being with your animals. You don't plan it out. You just do it. And you probably could write a book about animals and horse training.

The problem with all of us is usually that we think we have a problem. And we don't have a problem. To some part of yourself, it makes sense to be alone. You don't want a man messing with your life. I mean, to me, that makes totally logical sense. You've finally decided where you want to sit. And you're like a novelist who's just finished a novel but doesn't want to finish the last page because that's when you submit it to the publishers and they say, "We like it" or "We don't like it. You've got to change this."

And that's what brings us to the shadow side of Quantum Affirmations, because when you have that relationship, when you have that wonderful future that you're going to have, you'll be worried about losing it. There's no two ways about it; it just, as I say, comes with the territory. So we can do that with eyes closed again.

So this is the Quantum Affirmation that has to do with the final process, which is that "bright lights make shadows." So here we are in the house again; same place, same guy, same horse hanging out outside waiting for the kids to bring carrots and sugar. And it's really a great time.

And you're looking around and you're seeing all this love and light, and these children are bringing you so much joy. And you're worried about their future. And you're worried about your husband's health, and you're worried about your health. And you're worried about life. And you're worried about the horse. These are things that are going to happen, because with this beautiful, wonderful future will come the fear of losses, as it is with anyone who has anything.

So you can say to yourself, "Just like I can handle this horse if this horse got crazy, just like I can handle these crazy kids and this husband, I can handle what life brings." And you're telling your subconscious, "I can handle this. Don't keep it away from me because I'm afraid of it. I can handle this, and this is the future that I want. This is the quantum future that I want."

In quantum physics, there's something called "quantum tunneling," and this little electron can go instantaneously through the most gigantic barriers by quantum tunneling. And love and life and the real stuff are not local. They're not dependent on time. They're not dependent on anything, and they last forever, and this is now connecting you to that future, and in that future, you're dealing with a new set of problems that comes with you attracting your quantum future…And now you can open your eyes.

Meg: Six Weeks After Our Initial Session

MONTE: I'm here with Meg; it's six weeks later. And we're here to discuss how Quantum Affirmations has changed your life. When you've been doing your Quantum Affirmations, have you noticed any changes in your life?

MEG: I have. I have, a lot, actually. Mainly that it's kept my goals in the forefront. You know, for years it was sort of suppressed, and there'd always be work and other priorities that would come into play, so by the discipline of the Quantum Affirmations and being disciplined about doing them for the morning and the night, at the very least it's been keeping this issue in the forefront, so I'm having direct actions.

MONTE: It makes perfect sense. What we were talking about six weeks ago was you were looking to meet somebody, whether to have a permanent relationship or fun with; you know that's the term of our reality, and you had identified various issues that you felt were holding you back. Have you had any progress in any of those issues?

MEG: I have indirectly. I've found that I had some really big health issues that I had to deal with, so it was good to have to deal with it and get that out of the way, so to speak. And I feel a lot, lot better, and I've had some weight loss as a result of it, and we'll have some more to look forward to hopefully with these issues now.

MONTE: I do remember that was one of the issues that you felt that you had since moving to this area. You put on weight and you thought that that might be impacting your ability to attract somebody, so the universe has obviously worked in a very odd way, which it often does to conspire with you, to help you lose weight. So did you actually lose pounds or …?

MEG: Six pounds so far. In four weeks.

MONTE: That's a lot! That's a healthy way to do it; that's the way it stays off.

MEG: Yes. The doctor was very happy with that and I'm very happy with that, so I'll keep on track.

MONTE: You changed your diet because of the health issue.

MEG: A drastic change of diet. And a drastic change of lifestyle is going to have to come into play, too—how we structure my whole summer. Working seven days a week from morning to night can no longer happen.

MONTE: Interesting.

MEG: So now I'm going to have to be almost normal, so to speak, whatever that is.

MONTE: Well, that's the Quantum Affirmations; it's about describing the new normal for you.

MEG: Right. So be it a day off or being done with work by five or six o'clock in the evening instead of working till nine o'clock or ten o'clock at night, every night, I'm hoping that it will increase my chances of meeting someone, whether it is pumping gas or going to the Starbucks...

MONTE: So it seems like the Quantum Affirmations has had quite an impact. Of course, someone could also say that these were issues that were waiting to happen, but you are able to address them easier because you felt more in control. Why do you think that some of these changes happened? What sent you to the doctor?

MEG: I was having some pain that I was ignoring for quite a while, actually.

MONTE: So you're more in your body as a result—not necessarily doing the Quantum Affirmations, but you're more in your body and more listening to your body.

MEG: More aware of things. More aware of things or, I should say, less likely to ignore them.

MONTE: That's one of the things that I've always enjoyed about this way of living, which I call Quantum Affirmations, but it's really what Amy and I evolved as just a way of responding to life. It does make you very aware of what's going on. You try to take care of yourself because you're so aware of it. So you were actually so in your head, thinking about what was going on, that you weren't listening to your body.

MEG: For years.

MONTE: Really?

MEG: Maybe fifteen, twenty years or so.

MONTE: Well then, forgive me for taking the liberty of telling you what's going on with you, but it seems like you're in more of a balanced state between head, heart, and what we call your home, your body. That's the best way to bring you to balance, to magnetize yourself to bring your Quantum Affirmations to life. When you did it, can you describe the actual process of what you would see and how you would get to the point of where you're seeing or feeling or hearing anything?

MEG: Well, it wasn't easy at first. There are lots of distractions, so it's a little bit hard to really tune things out and quiet your mind.

MONTE: Especially when you have a lot of animals running around.

MEG: Precisely. But I got increasingly better and better about being able to just quiet my mind and see clear pictures of what I want, and it's amazing how then those clear pictures end up becoming clearer as time goes on and easier to manifest. And it's a short period of time, never more than five or ten minutes.

MONTE: It shouldn't be.

MEG: Never more, yes. And my mind wanders after that time anyway. And then actually—recently I've had a really big breakthrough; it's been very easy to be able to get into that spot and very much quiet my mind and go into this very deep, quiet place for few minutes and be able to focus on that.

MONTE: That's great, and that will be great for your healing, too. Because the heart is the only thing we can consciously control and we do that by controlling the breath, and when you do the Quantum Affirmations and it calms you down, that's when healing can take place on all levels, physical and spiritual.

MEG: Right.

MONTE: So did you hear things mainly or do you see things mainly, or did you ever smell things or did you bring up things from the past?

MEG: I see very clear pictures and hear things. I never smell anything, and generally the pictures are those that just start expanding, and it's amazing what pops into your head, other repetitive things that pop into your head. Just all of the happiness and the fulfillment involved with seeing pictures of a husband and children, and all of those good things.

MONTE: And did you have the negative intrude, which I always do whenever I'm envisioning something that's coming up in the future, because I'm actually at this point of doing Quantum Affirmations, looking for what's going to be the negative part of the new reality that I'm trying to make for myself because I know that will help me make it real. Did you ever see a husband who might be doing something you don't want him to do, or coming home late or… ?

MEG: No, but I had doubts about the process at one point.

MONTE: What?

MEG: When is it going to happen? The impatience: "Okay, all right, fine, it's just fun," but you know. And then the more you get into it, the more the anxiety goes away and you see how things suited me to align, I guess. You have some sort of faith in the process as far as that goes, but of course there's doubt.

MONTE: Well, you have the hardest one because your Quantum Affirmations involves another person. So there's only so much you can do, but what you're doing is making yourself into the person that you want to be, and that's the person that's going to attract the person you want to attract. Because when you feel the best about yourself, that's when you'll attract the right person.

MEG: And for me my weight is very much a part of it and the state of my business. It's very important for me to be whatever the interpretation of a successful person is. That's an important part of my makeup from my self-esteem. That's the basis of it, so that's the key for me, I suppose, to not come to a relationship feeling like I'm the weakest part of the equation.

MONTE: It makes sense. You want to feel good about yourself, and on every level. And you want to be bringing things to the relationship and not looking to the relationship to save you. That's one of the things that sabotages so many people in their relationships. They're expecting the other person to complete them or to save them, or magically change their life. And you're working on magically changing your life from Quantum Affirmations so that they don't have to. So now the part of your life with your partner can be the fun and fulfilling partnership part.

MEG: Right. And then a lot of my affirmations go to the joy of raising children together. That's a lot of my visions. Because that really is what pair bonding is all about to me. . . I mean the enjoyment of raising these people into being adults.

MONTE: That's cool. So you see yourself with little babies?

MEG: Yes.

MONTE: That's exciting!

MEG: And of course the horses and the animals. It all comes into the picture.

MONTE: It sounds very beautiful!

MEG: It is, yes. It's really great.

MONTE: Sounds like a greeting card.

MEG: Yes, it is.

Meg: Twelve Weeks After Our First Session

MEG: My "twelve weeks later" has been life changing on so many levels. The simple act of doing my Quantum Affirmations has translated to a great amount of positive action in my life. I look forward to those five to ten minutes of the Quantum Affirmations at the start and end of my day. They bring to me a peace of mind, knowing that the love of my life is out there with the quality of the family life I have always dreamed of, being completely attainable. I feel that my level of anxiety in general has diminished and the blocks I put in place to prevent what I want more than anything are being dealt with. I have lost twenty pounds; my general health and my professional life have improved enormously. What I am most surprised by the effect of the Quantum Affirmations is my ability to live more in the now by having hope and faith in the future. Thank you, Monte, for all of your guidance.

CHAPTER 13

CASE STUDY
QUANTUM AFFIRMATION FOR WEIGHT LOSS—COLETTE

Colette: Before

MONTE: So what's brought you here today to talk about Quantum Affirmations?

COLETTE: Well, I think I've reached a plateau in weight loss and I would really like to lose thirty-five to forty pounds.

MONTE: Okay, that's a good goal. So in Quantum Affirmations, the first thing you would do would be to analyze your question and your goal, because the ancients had a saying: "If you know your question, you know your answer." The process of delving into why you're asking what you're asking and refining your question will sometimes lead you to breakthroughs that can sometimes even negate the necessity for going even further. But this is a very big problem. I myself have had this problem. I could say I have it right now. The first thing to look at is, Why do you want to lose weight when you look fine the way you are? Do you want to lose weight because some other person is judging, or are you judging yourself to other people?

COLETTE: Well, I think that at this weight, there is something limiting. I think I'm limiting myself. I think I'm limiting my abundance of health. I think I'm limiting how I feel about myself sometimes as a woman. I wind up judging myself going out the door, and sometimes I'll look at my hips or I'll look at my backside and I'm thinking, well, if I was just a few pounds thinner, I'd feel more comfortable in my skin. So I'd like to feel more comfortable in my skin and a little bit more graceful when I walk through the door and a little lighter and have less judgment on myself.

MONTE: If you're not feeling well and you think it's related to weight, and if a doctor says it's related to weight, that makes a lot of sense. But in terms of judging yourself, I think that's a very important issue with Quantum Affirmations, because in Quantum Affirmations, we're going to get into a purity that every actor looks for. Quantum Affirmations is acting as if what you want is existing right now. When it comes down to wanting to look a certain way, then the next question that you ask, since we're at the goal stage of Quantum Affirmations, is, Why do you want to look that way? You said it's because you are judging yourself. But by whose standard are you judging yourself? Once again, if it's a physical health issue, that makes perfect sense, and then we don't even have to look any further.

But once judgment comes into play, we need to look further. Let's say, if you hadn't come here today to talk about weight, you'd come to talk about love. The person who loves you doesn't care about what you're talking about. They love you the way you are right now. The Quantum Affirmation you do for someone you love would be for someone who loves you exactly the way you are. If you want to change, they're there to help you. If you don't want to change, that's fine; you are the way you were when they met you. So that's what I'm trying to apply to this particular case—that Quantum Affirmations is a lifelong goal, a lifelong exercise, and it cuts across all the different desires that we all have.

So how do you react when I say that about your experience of going out of the house and judging yourself in terms of trying to attract someone or to bring love into your life? How would you feel if that person met you and just liked you the way you were?

COLETTE: That's so interesting that you say that, because I often feel that my extra weight, my extra pounds, are very insulating, and it's almost like I'm creating a barrier about people coming into my life.

MONTE: Well, you're attractive anyway. So you're saying that if you were to lose the weight, you would then attract all the people who weren't willing to break through, to see past the cultural conditioning about how a woman is supposed to look, like the waifs that adorn the magazines. So you're creating what they call in business a "barrier to entry" for the person that you are trying to attract; they have to get past that and they have to want to get to know the real you. Tell your subconscious that that feeling of your heart opening is about the future that you want, not the feeling of your fist clenching. Because even though sometimes people say, "I want this," they don't really want this. A lot of people will come to me for love, but they're happy the way they are. They don't want some guy or some girl coming in and messing up their life and saying, "Clean up the house," or "You've got to" do this or that, or feeling like "I've got to put on my makeup for this person instead of just going around the way I want." So it's all about truth, being a truth seeker. You said your Native American name was...

COLETTE: Shadow Seeker.

MONTE: So obviously you're going to do very well with this process. Plus you're a great mother...

COLETTE: I'm a great advocate. I have advocated for three children with disabilities, and they have all been mainstreamed, graduating with honors from college and doing phenomenally well.

MONTE: That's amazing. You have the kinds of gifts and the kinds of skills and that which flows effortlessly and endlessly to you that are the kinds of things that everybody else would want, and weight loss is just another aspect of something that can certainly flow. If you can do that, you can do THAT. Quantum Affirmations is all about peeling the onion of resistance to the future that you say you want. We all know what happens when we peel an onion: We cry.

COLETTE: Yes.

MONTE: So it's all about getting through the tears that are going to come with the new future.

COLETTE: But the tears are a lack of control. At this weight, at this part of my life, I have a modicum of control. I know how people are going to respond to me right now. But if I'm thirty or forty or fifty pounds thinner, where's that control?

MONTE: You'll have to get a new level of control, and that's a part of your Quantum Affirmation. We did the visualization where you closed your eyes and saw the future. But Quantum Affirmations is really an eyes-open meditation as well. Because you can feel exactly what it would feel like, especially you who has had acting training, can feel exactly what it's like to be that person, the thirty-pounds-less person. Because when you do acting, you are another person. So you're that person now. Do you feel out of control?

COLETTE: No.

MONTE: Okay. Why would you think you'd be out of control? See, this visualization is real. We're here. We're in that future now. We're quantum entangled with the future.

COLETTE: Because I feel safe with you. There's safety with some-one that you know is kind and you're friends with. There is safety there.

MONTE: I understand completely. So let's try the classic visual-ization method, which is to close your eyes, see yourself in the future that you want to be in. You're now thirty pounds lighter, or however much lighter, with the size jeans that you have; your goal jeans are now on you; you're wearing them. You look fantastic. You walk into a place that you're accustomed to being. You're with people that you're accustomed to being with. How are they reacting?

COLETTE: They're amazed, and they're saying—"COLETTE, you look great! You look great!" And...

MONTE: Are they really happy for you?

COLETTE: No.

MONTE: Are some of them really happy for you?

COLETTE: Yes.

MONTE: Those are your friends.

COLETTE: Yes.

MONTE: So unfortunately, part of the Quantum Affirmation and part of the brutal honest truth that you have to have when either doing psychic readings or really trying to change your-self in a serious way is that you have to realize that when you change yourself, you are going to lose friends—because these are not your friends. These are people that are with you because you have shared issues. They're not ready to share pure love with you. The people who love you, love you no matter how you look. If, God forbid, you lost various parts of your body, they'd love you just as much. These are the people you want to be with. You don't want to be with the people who are false friends. And in the Quantum Affirmation, now you can see yourself shedding—as well as the weight—shedding these people who, God bless them, have their issues, and we have our issues right now. But they won't be in your life. There's a really good chance they won't be in your life. But knowing you, you'll probably do something to make them feel better like, "Don't worry, I lost the weight; But I'll gain the weight again." That's what you've got to be very careful about, because you love them so much that you're even willing to go against what your best interest is.

COLETTE: But do I really love them, or am I just comfortable?

MONTE: Well, you're quantum entangled with them. Quantum entanglement works in the present moment as well. Once you have enmeshed yourself with somebody—that's what the psychologists call it; in quantum physics, it's entanglement—once you're enmeshed with someone, you would worry about what they feel to the point where you're willing to sacrifice yourself for them. And unfortunately, you have a family that you have to depend on first for that kind of information. But even then, it's not right for you to do anything negative to yourself, because the first rule of warfare is "Make your base secure," according to Colonel Carl von Clauswitz (1780—1831), the father of modern warfare.

So by doing Quantum Affirmations and becoming the person that you really, at essence, want to be after you've gotten through all the reasons—you are now secure. You can help your son. You can help your other son. You can help your daughter. You can help anyone who deserves help. If you're just like, "Oh my God! They're not feeling well. I'm going to sacrifice myself and I'm going to gain the weight or lose the weight or I'm going to do this for them so that they're not uncomfortable because I look so much prettier than they are and so that they don't worry that I'm going to steal their boyfriends or their husbands." There are millions of reasons.

But once you're doing life tough—you know, it's like the way the prisoners talk about it: "I'm going to do my time hard." They're going to do hard times. They're going to get through it. Once you decide, "I'm going to be who I really am," you will find love, and money will flow more easily because you're not putting your energy into these waves of quantum energy that are not designed to push you forward. They're designed to keep you where you are.

You don't want to be quantum entangled with people in the present who aren't ready to help you. So now we can close our eyes again. This is the classic way of doing visualization. You could either see it as Shakespeare put it so beautifully, "in your mind's eye," or you can see it on a screen; you can see it anyway you want. But now see yourself going to a new place with no one that you know. It could be a social situation, and here you are, looking the way you want to look. How you do feel in this visualization?

COLETTE: Wonderful.

MONTE: Cool. Now all these guys are coming up to talk to you, and a few girls. How do you feel now? Because you like to make people feel good, remember? You've got to be careful with it, because these guys want you to make them feel good. But they might have a definition that's different from the one you have. You're a loving person. So will it help you in your life to lose this weight, or will it confuse the way things are going for you?

COLETTE: It will help me get to my other goals.

MONTE: Yes, because I see it helping you. As a psychic, I see that you will take to this like a duck to water and that you'll be the same person but you will have to just have a different type of—you said before the word *threat* is what came to you, and that's totally logical, smart. You will just have to have a different level of what the government calls *threat assessment*. You will have to be a little more suspicious of why people are talking to you and what they're saying.

We're not doing the Quantum Affirmations program for money right now, but it all applies; each one applies to everyone. I read for a lot of wealthy people. One of their issues is that they can't tell who's interested in them because of their money and who's interested because of who they really are. And I'm sure you have this already because you are an attractive person. You can't tell if they're talking to you because you're attractive or because they really want to get to know you, so your threat assessment's going to be different in this visualization. You know, as I've been talking, I'm sure you're seeing a whole movie in there. So can you share some of that with us?

COLETTE: Yes, what I was seeing is that as a performer, as an actor, that many people have put limits on me because of my weight, because they want a different type, a certain type. And that if I lose that weight, I'll have many more opportunities to be on stage or to do other things in acting and in the arts and how that will open my life up. I also saw it as being stronger as a person and developing healthy boundaries, not barriers and not an arsenal of weapons, but healthy boundaries of being able to say no to certain things and not having to be always so nice. I could say no.

MONTE: I love it. That was very powerful. Those are like a cannon shot.

Colette: Six Weeks After Our Initial Session

MONTE: How much have you lost?

COLETTE: Well, in about six weeks, I lost about eight and a half, nine pounds.

MONTE: That's great. I can see it.

COLETTE: Oh, thank you.

MONTE: Since your Quantum Affirmations is about a subject that generates about a hundred thousand books a decade and incredible amounts of money spent by people, what's your secret? Was Quantum Affirmations part of your weight-loss program?

COLETTE: Well, I'm in my forties and having to deal with weight-loss issues where the weight just doesn't want to come off and trying to just accept myself where I was, but still needing to lose some weight, I found it to be a struggle until I started utilizing the tools you gave me.

MONTE: I see.

COLETTE: What I found very interesting was the first week of using the tools of Quantum Affirmations, I felt that my choices were very bold choices but very significant. If I wanted to have something that wasn't a diet food, I was going to just enjoy it and not judge myself on it.

MONTE: Right. Because we did see at that time six weeks ago that that was one of the issues—how uncomfortable you would feel with your body and how uncomfortable you'd feel in your body and what you put into it in terms of control and how people would see you. It sounds like you are accepting yourself more.

COLETTE: Well, the interesting thing about accepting myself more, accepting being a full human being, was that the choices I was making were about being aware about what I was eating. I wasn't eating unconsciously, like in front of the TV or something like that. It was a conscious choice, and what I did have, I enjoyed. But it was just enjoying it. Then I made other different choices during the week. I started going on the treadmill and I started measuring food. I thought, "Well, I want to enjoy this, but I'm just going to measure. I'm not going to deny myself."

MONTE: Good.

COLETTE: I thought, "I'm just going to measure things," and then I didn't have to measure it. I was able to say, "Okay, well, this is about a cup," and in just over these six weeks, without really trying, I have to say that it wasn't really a Herculean effort. It was about choosing what I wanted, and then I enjoyed it. It wasn't about denial or hurting myself or "food is bad." It was about enjoying the moment.

MONTE: It seems like you were yourself all throughout the day. This is how it's seeming to me from the outside, as a lot of times when we eat unconsciously—like you said, in front of the television—we're sort of not ourselves; we're distracted. But it seems like you were conscious and present more during the day than most people are, because a lot of people do eat reflexively. When you did your Quantum Affirmation, did you do it in the morning, or did you do it at night, or did you do it before you ate? How did you do it?

COLETTE: I did it at night so when I woke up I had done the entire programming at night. I did my meditation and I did my Quantum Affirmations, so when I started the day, I started my day with a purpose.

MONTE: Wow, that's great!

COLETTE: It wasn't "Okay, I have to go take the kids to the bus stop and run here and run errands." It was, "I'm going to enjoy myself."

MONTE: Wow, this is very powerful thing you're saying, because as the Dalai Lama says, "The purpose of life is to be happy." This is something a lot of people forget, and they think that the purpose of life is to be serious or to accomplish various things. But you're applying happiness to all aspects of your life including eating, whereas before eating might have been something that you were conflicted about. Did you see things from the past? When you were visualizing your new future, the new place where you're going to plant your quantum flag, did you see any particular thing happening that has happened, or have you seen anything that has not happened that you wanted to happen?

COLETTE: I saw something very interesting. What a great thing to bring up! Because what I saw happened was that certain people were threatened even by an eight-pound or ten-pound weight loss.

MONTE: I remember that was one of the issues. So in other words, you saw that in your Quantum Affirmations and then you actually saw it in real life.

COLETTE: Actually, people in my family were bringing home some of the foods that I would normally love to snack on, thinking that they were treating me. "Oh, here's a treat for you." And it was almost sabotage, because at that moment I

wasn't going to enjoy it because it would have been unconscious eating for me. It would have been, "Okay, I'm just
going to eat it to make someone else happy, because that's
what they brought for me." That was a different kind of thing,
that aspect of being threatened, that their security felt a little
off. But that's okay, because they're choosing to grow, too.

MONTE: Yes, and they mean well. Everybody wants things to
stay the same, because they pretty much can handle what's
going on and you don't know what the future's going to be.
That's when everyone gets nervous, when the future's coming
up. So you're leading by example, showing them that you
can take this kind of change and this kind of power. When
someone is powerful—and this was one of your issues; I
remembered you didn't want to show people how powerful
you were by taking control of your eating—you're showing
people how powerful you are because this is an issue for so
many people in the world. There are even people who want to
gain weight, and so food is at the same point a different kind
of issue.

So you had people bringing you things; they mean well.
This is one of the interesting threats that seem to be running through all the Quantum Affirmations: how people
are allowing or not allowing the world to affect them. One
of the things that I've been the most pleased hearing is that
people are allowing the world to affect them in the sense that
it confronts their Quantum Affirmations, so that there's more
consciousness. It sounds like there's a lot of consciousness in
your living now.

COLETTE: Exactly, exactly. The primary goal was taking control and the respect of claiming my power.

MONTE: Right.

COLETTE: That was taking control of my personal power. The secondary gain of that was that everyone's commented on how much happier I am.

MONTE: Oh, that's wonderful.

COLETTE: They say things like, "Colette, you're glowing."

MONTE: You are.

COLETTE: It was wonderful. It's a comment that I'm getting all the time now, and I find myself sharing little bits and pieces of what I'm doing, and people are coming away saying, "Wow, this is really something to look at." So I'm having a very positive experience.

MONTE: That's wonderful. You couldn't make me any happier, because what you're doing is something that I myself have had to do, and it's something that so many people have to do. So Quantum Affirmations can actually help you lose weight.

COLETTE: Well, I'm living proof.

Colette: Twelve Weeks After Our First Session

COLETTE: My "twelve-weeks-later" phase is quite astounding. I am still empowered and losing weight. Interestingly enough, my focus has been shifted to removing blockages to personal success. I had a longing to make really good theater. My dream is to make people laugh and feel good. Yet, life events seemed to block every attempt at making that happen. I began applying Quantum Affirmations to my goal. I saw myself on stage, hearing the applause and laughter, and working with great actors. I also saw the hard work and commitment it would take. I shared my dream with actors that I trusted, and they were inspired. Flying Monkey Players are now in rehearsal! We are in the middle of producing a great play. The main theme is "love conquers all." This is something I had only dreamed about, and now that dream is a reality. Thank you, Monte, for making my dreams come true!

CHAPTER 14

Q...U...A...N...T...U...M

The seven steps below offer some guidance for increasing the effectiveness of your Quantum Affirmations.

Q—BE QUIET: Always do your Quantum Affirmations at a time and in a place where you will not be disturbed. Removing or altering ingrained habits takes time and patient practice at as regular a time as possible. Be patient—that is a master habit that heals. Be patient with yourself, with others, and with the invisible forces that surround and sustain you. Quiet your mind. Calm and center yourself. Take a few deep breaths . . . in and out . . . slowly, to center yourself. Focus your thoughts on the new Quantum Reality that you are in.

U—BE UNATTACHED: When you do your quantumplaytion, it is especially helpful to affirm that everything in the universe is connected but unfolds in perfect divine order. Do not be attached to a time factor or to a particular way for your goal to be realized. Allow your desires to unfold in the perfect time and manner. Be certain that you will reach your goal while letting go of expectations as to how and when it will happen. All expectations are unreasonable. No one is guaranteed another breath, let alone winning the lottery. When we have expectations and become attached to them, we can block the natural flow of energy. Often you will receive something even better or more appropriate than you wished for.

A—BE APPRECIATIVE: Express gratitude for all that you have. You cannot allow yourself the luxury of a negative thought about where you are now, because those doubts will impede your intention to manifest what you want. When you are thankful and feel fulfilled now, your goal will manifest much more easily. What we focus on in our mind's eye is ultimately reflected back to us in our experience of reality. If you let go of situations and attitudes that no longer serve your higher good, then you can grow and expand on many levels. You can create what you want by using the power of affirmation. Remember, you may have been programming yourself with negative affirmations for many years, and it will take a little while to get you back on track.

N—BE NOURISHED: Whatever your desires, stating your clear Quantum Affirmation and allying yourself with nurturing, like-minded people can accelerate the results. Don't "cast your pearls before swine." Do not share what you have learned in this book with anyone you are not certain will be supportive. Even supportive people will give you their opinions, so you may just want to keep your efforts to yourself. If you accept the premise that everything in the universe is somehow connected, even though we can't always see that connection, you then realize that you are not separate from your desire and can fully embrace it. Nourish yourself with positive energy wherever you can find it, to encourage and strengthen you. Surround yourself with images and ideas that help you to become clear about your intention, in the safe place you do your Quantum Affirmation, at your place of work, or wherever appropriate.

T—BE TRUSTING: Once you've set an intention, it's time for trust and faith to set in. But it takes practice to develop your manifesting skills to the level where you can learn to trust them. Have faith in the process, and know that the universe is working its magic. You don't need anyone's permission to do this. Practice makes perfect. Expect the gift. Accept it. Love the feeling of having what you desire. Intend that your goal manifest in a manner that is for your highest good and greatest joy. This is very important, as intentions that are created out of desperation, fear of failure, or ego issues will backfire. You may get what you want, but it will disappoint. Alternatively, you may get the exact opposite of what you want. But intentions that are genuinely made for your highest good and greatest joy tend to manifest in a positive way.

U—BE UNBLOCKED: Do you feel you are truly worthy and that you deserve to manifest your goal? Often an intention may be blocked energetically by an underlying belief that it is not in your best interest. If the desired result hasn't appeared in your life, there may be a block to clear. Some people have a prejudice against success, thus instinctually repelling desired goals from their lives. When you are conflicted in your thoughts, you will manifest obstacles. Do you have space energetically to receive your desire into your daily experience? Sometimes receiving your intention may disrupt your life, and subconsciously a part of you could be repelling it. Everyone gets tested on expanding their ability to receive. Experience yourself receiving your intention, know that you are deserving, and create an opening of space inside of yourself for your desire to come into your life.

M—BE MINDFUL: To give is to receive. To receive is to give. This follows from a oneness that is at the core of my Quantum Affirmations process. Counter to our thinking in the world of separation, when you give you do not lose what you give; rather, you receive more of what you give. Your thoughts help to create your life experiences. We all create our own journey using our thoughts. We all use the same "stuff" to create our life experiences. That "stuff" is Universal or Source Energy. There is enough for everyone to have a wonderful life. Our thoughts draw and shape raw Source Energy into a myriad of forms that we observe each day. We all draw from the one and the same source of energy. Be aware and be mindful.

CHAPTER 15

THE 36 QUANTUM ASPIRATIONS TO HELP YOU STAY FOCUSED IN DAILY LIFE

Quantum Affirmations should be done at a time and place where you know you won't be disturbed and where you can feel safe and secure enough to concentrate fully your relaxed attention on visualizing completely your new Quantum Reality. But what about when you stop Quantum Affirming and your present reality becomes your focus, as it should be?

The following affirmations, which I call my Quantum Aspirations, are designed to help you counteract the "negative" affirmations that may arise in you as you face the many challenges of even the most uneventful day. Think of them as a virtual pack of breath mints for your mind when it gets a little stale and unpleasant in there and you need a fresh perspective lest you offend someone and embarrass yourself with unconscious behavior (that makes perfect sense to some crazy part of you, remember?). You would be amazed if you could see a replay of all the seemingly insignificant moments that affected your life profoundly for good or ill. Keeping a clear head by using my Quantum Aspirations will keep you alert, centered, and focused on the present moment and the people you are with. Never forget that the people you are with are people, too, not cardboard cutouts or the actors in your quantumplaytions. The golden rule of "Do unto others as you would have others do unto you" always applies, and so does one or more of my Quantum Aspirations. They are a little bonus gift to you as a token of my appreciation for taking the Quantum Affirmations journey with me.

(1) **I experience my emotions and channel them into useful actions.**

Use this affirmation when passions flare or strong feelings threaten to overwhelm logic and practicality. Experience emotions honestly as they arise; do not suppress them. The negative ones will subside over time in the light of reason and compassion for yourself and others. What you are passionate about can show you the way to change your life.

(2) **I enjoy being independent and taking care of myself.**

Use this affirmation when you are lonely or feel overly dependent upon or let down by people and circumstances. The best partnerships are the union of self-reliant people who know themselves well and seek to understand and support each other in all ways. If you cannot have that, you are better off being on your own. It will prepare you for new partnerships.

(3) **I invent creative solutions to all challenges in my life.**

Use this affirmation when you are confronted with a situation that seems impossible to deal with. Sometimes it is better to study a problem until you understand it well and then put it out of your mind for a while. Many scientists and mathematicians have reported that their inventions and creative solutions came to them in a dream or the reverie of a daydream.

(4) **The riches of the world come to me effortlessly.**

Use this affirmation when you believe that you are poor, that you are working too hard, or that nothing comes easily for you. Too many people believe the negative affirmation that nothing good can come into their life without lots of hard work, sacrifice, and suffering. Replace that negative affirmation with this one and enjoy yourself more. You deserve the best.

(5) **I am patient in the face of delay and obstacles.**

Use this affirmation when you are upset because you or another person is late or stuck in traffic or when encountering other situations that you obviously cannot do anything about at the time. Patience is a great teacher, a sign of maturity and wisdom. If we approach them with calm and patience, difficult situations have a remarkable way of eventually working out.

(6) I have all that I need to get what I want.

Use this affirmation when you believe you lack the time, money, IQ, education, connections, looks, love, strength, prestige, power, luck, support, courage, patience, or any other resources you need to accomplish your goal. Believe, instead, that the power of affirmations and positive thinking can help you as much as all these things combined.

(7) I learn from mistakes and grow wise and strong.

Use this affirmation when you are angry with yourself or other people for having made what you consider to be a mistake. All expectations are unreasonable, especially the expectation that you can go through life without making mistakes and having to deal with the mistakes of others. Successful people know mistakes are valuable learning experiences.

(8) I am flexible and can adapt to the challenges of our "now age."

Use this affirmation when information overload, constant change, and other aspects of the rapid pace of modern life threaten to overwhelm you. Modern "conveniences" have eliminated the cushion of time necessary to properly absorb and consider information and concepts. To achieve true knowledge and wisdom, you must take time each day for quiet reflection.

(9) I control my life with the decisions that I make.

Use this affirmation when you believe your life is out of your control. The root cause of most problems is poor decision making. Take responsibility for your life. Your present situation is the result of your past decisions. You can get where you want to be by making better decisions. Using an oracle, one of mine or those of others, can help you develop your decision-making ability.

(10) **I defend and protect myself and those I care for.**

Use this affirmation when you feel that your best interests and the best interests of those you care about are being threatened. Stand up for what you know is right. There is no reason that you and those you care about should suffer due to the ignorance, poor decision making, or malicious intent of anyone. Those who are wrong need to be shown their error.

(11) **I learn valuable lessons from studying the past.**

Use this affirmation when you are not satisfied with your life or are tormented by how different you believe things could and should have been "if only . . ." The present moment is your only point of power. Taking action now in harmony with what you know you have to do, while using the past to guide your actions, is the best way to change your future.

(12) **I forgive myself and all those trying to grow.**

Use this affirmation whenever you get down on yourself or others—especially when you notice the use of negative affirmations. Be happy that you notice these things; it means you are making fast progress. Loving yourself and others requires forgiveness; it is an essential quality of the truly successful person living a life of quality and meaning.

(13) **I am a good leader because I know how to follow.**

Use this affirmation whenever you must organize or guide others or must speak in public. If you put the needs of the group ahead of your own needs, you will do well. If you have trouble with authority figures, you will not be comfortable being one. Good leaders and good speakers know what they want to communicate and then do so clearly and succinctly.

(14) **I surround myself with beauty and positive people.**

Use this affirmation when the world seems a frightening place or when people refuse to support you in your positive efforts. Remember, your actions to improve yourself are threatening to those who want to control you or resist improving themselves. Use beautiful art, music, and creativity of all kinds to remind you how wonderful and enjoyable life is.

(15) **I deserve love and respect because I give them.**

Use this affirmation when you feel you are not getting the love and respect you need and deserve. If you are able to show your love and respect for others, there is no reason why they should not do the same to you. You are not being egotistical to demand respect. This affirmation can empower you to tell others how you feel in an appropriate manner.

(16) **I enjoy exercising, eating healthy foods, and doing what is good for me.**

Use this affirmation when you feel resistant to doing what you know is in your best interests. The desire to sabotage our efforts to improve ourselves comes from our resistance to change and to being "too good." With self-improvement come new activities, friends, and other manifestations of change we so often resist because we fear the unknown.

(17) **I use criticism only for making things better.**

Use this affirmation when you are either the user or the recipient of criticism that is meant to tear down rather than build up. We must be truthful with ourselves and others. We cannot improve unless we are able to see what needs improvement. However, when we forget to turn off our critical faculty, we become someone who is neither happy nor fun to be with.

(18) **I am free of pain and suffering.**

Use this affirmation to remember who you really are. Breathe slowly and deeply as you remember you are a soul moving onward and upward. You are not your name. You are not what you do. You are not your body. Visualize beautiful birds removing your pain and suffering with their golden beaks and flying away to drop them in the vast ocean.

(19) **I am attractive because I feel good about myself and others.**

Use this affirmation when you are unhappy with your appearance. Everyone needs to use this affirmation several times a day. Even classically beautiful people obsess over what they see as their physical shortcomings. A thoughtful, kind person who is genuinely interested in others is truly attractive. A sense of humor is also more important than "good" looks.

(20) **I am content in all circumstances.**

Use this affirmation whenever you notice you are discontent with things the way they are. Try instead believing that things are the way they are now for a reason you do not know yet. What is important now is not that you perfectly attain or maintain this exalted state, but how quickly you return to trying to attain it when you notice yourself forgetting to try.

(21) **I create partnerships that are fair and pleasurable.**

Use this affirmation when you are lonely or when existing relationships are unsatisfying. Partners you bring into your life are living manifestations of what you believe are the answer to your own needs for growth and completion. If you believe you need to be aggressive, defensive, or alone to become yourself fully, you will manifest that in your daily life.

(22) **I take my time and rest, relax, and rejuvenate.**

Use this affirmation when you are hurried, pressured, or overworked or believe you cannot take any time for yourself. No matter what your situation, you will handle any challenge better if you are well rested, fit, and healthy and if you take the time to do the job correctly. Do not let exhaustion and self-denial turn into an accident, injury, or disease. Enjoy life more.

(23) **I am positive that I have the power to transform my life.**

Use this affirmation when you notice resistance, either in yourself or in others, to the idea of your being able to use your Quantum Affirmations practice to help you change your life. Profound change usually comes in small increments over time. Keep a positive attitude and you will be able to undo years of negative affirmations in record time.

(24) **My willpower is stronger than my bad habits.**

Use this affirmation when you feel unable to overcome long-held beliefs, habits, and compulsions. Like affirmations, our habits' strength comes from constant repetition and our belief in their ability to help us cope with life in some way. They can be dealt with by using this gift and by accepting and loving yourself more and more, shadow side and all.

(25) **I appreciate all that I have and have accomplished.**

Use this affirmation when you notice yourself being envious or resentful of others. If you think negatively toward those who have what you believe you lack, you will program your subconscious mind to prevent you from becoming one of them. Know that they, too, have sacrificed and worked for what they have. Admire them for their accomplishments.

(26) **I am open to new ideas, techniques, and people.**

Use this affirmation when you notice you are resistant to allowing the possibility that new ways of doing things and other people might have something to contribute to your life and to the attaining of your goal. No one knows it all. It is not weakness, but the greatest strength to know your limits and to get out of your own way and let others help you.

(27) **I make my highest ideals real by my actions.**

Use this affirmation when you notice you or someone else is not living up to the standards you have set for yourself and others. Forgive them and yourself for this and appreciate the fact that you noticed. We must be the agents of the changes we want to see happen in the world. Realize the truth of the old saying, "A good example is the best sermon."

(28) **I earn my living doing what I love.**

Use this affirmation when you feel unfulfilled by your present manner of employment. You created your present work situation and you can create a better one, too. Do work that nurtures your mind, body, and spirit and those of others. Whatever you do for a living, you can use your creativity to do it. Make your life a work of art and your art a work of life.

(29) **I accomplish anything I put my mind to.**

Use this affirmation when you doubt your intelligence, your memory, or your ability to achieve your goals. Your situation is largely the result of how well you blended your logical and intuitive faculties to direct your actions. Several times a day, focus with relaxed concentration on the mental image of that which you would like see come into being.

(30) **I believe in myself now, always, and in all ways.**

Use this affirmation when you feel like a failure or others seem to doubt your abilities. Your strengths and weaknesses are yours to experience and learn from in your own time. Accept yourself just as you are now, knowing that the mistakes you have made were helpers that guided the direction of your personal growth. It is never too late to change.

(31) **I discard what has outlived its usefulness.**

Use this affirmation when you are resisting letting go of outmoded ways of thinking and acting and people who are wasting your time, energy, and other resources. If you want new people, places, things, situations, and ideas to come to you, you must make room in your life for them. Then enjoy your new freedom and know exciting things are coming to you.

(32) **I love and accept myself as a unique individual.**

Use this affirmation when it seems that you are not being accepted for any reason, but especially if it is because you are different from other people or because you want to be different. You do not need the acceptance of ignorant or intolerant people. You cannot change anyone else. What you do need is to love and accept yourself for being a good person.

(33) I have faith in the future I cannot see.

Use this affirmation when you are worried or anxious. These feelings are usually caused by our attachment to a particular outcome happening a particular way or to wanting to know exactly how things are going to turn out. Though oracles can predict events with enough clarity to be helpful, we have the power to change our future. How many of your past worries never came to pass?

(34) I use my fears as signs that guide and protect me.

Use this affirmation when your fears prevent you from acting in your best interests. Our fears exist to help keep us safe from harm and from repeating mistakes we have made. If we seek to understand why we are afraid, we can make our fears our friend and helper, not our master. It is important to avoid fearing success and the many changes it will bring.

(35) I blend intuition and logic to guide my decisions.

Use this affirmation when you are having trouble making a decision. Usually, relying completely on either logic or intuition will not produce the most beneficial decisions. Assemble the facts and then review them as you ask the small voice of your intuition to guide you through feelings and hunches. If you are still not sure, it may be best not to decide yet.

(36) I have faith in miracles to bless and protect me.

Use this affirmation when life seems pointless or without hope. The realization that all things must end can sometimes make life seem not worth the effort. However, the miracles of our everyday life suggest other miracles that we are unaware of all around us.

About the Author

Photo: Amy Zerner

MONTE FARBER is an affirmations expert. He is the author of five successful affirmation decks (*Little Reminders: Love and Relationships*, *Little Reminders: Law of Attraction*, *The Healing Deck*, *Breathe Easy Deck*, and *Gifts of the Goddess Affirmation Cards*). He is also the author of a series of best-selling books, kits, and games illustrated by his wife, Amy Zerner, with whom he wrote *The Soulmate Path*, also published by Red Wheel/Weiser, along with their classic *Enchanted Tarot* book and Tarot deck set featuring seventy-eight of Amy's NEA award–winning fabric collage tapestries reproduced as the most beautiful and gentle deck available.

Virtually all of their more than forty titles incorporate the power of affirmations—designed to empower the reader by improving her or his intuition and decision-making ability—with more than two million copies of Monte's writings in print in fourteen languages. To learn more about Monte and Amy and their "spiritual power tools," including the CD of Monte leading you on several subject-driven guided Quantum Affirmations and the DVD containing the videos of Monte's actual counseling sessions with Michele, David, Meg, and Colette, visit www.TheEnchantedWorld.com. To learn more about Amy's inspirational art, Spiritual Couture™, and jewelry, visit www.AmyZerner.com.

Writing and inventing his many intuition-building works caused Monte to become quite psychic, a skill he employs professionally with an international client base through his Executive Strategic Planning Web site, www.ESPservices.net. He has appeared on a wide range of television and radio programs, including Home Shopping Network and QVC, where he and Amy were the first people in history to sell Tarot cards on television, and has done live readings over the air on venues as diverse as ABC and FOX News.

He has licensed six of his interactive personal guidance systems to www.myLifetime.com, Lifetime Television's Web site. Starting in 2008, Monte made uncannily accurate—more than 80 percent correct—psychic predictions about world events, the economy, and specific stocks every few months on dated-for-verification video clips in interviews by Alix Steele for Jim Cramer's financial Web site, www.TheStreet.com.

Living in the exclusive Hamptons area of Long Island, New York, Monte has personally counseled many celebrities and business elite, who know him as "The Best Astrologer in the Hamptons," a title bestowed upon him by Dan's Papers, for whose Web site he is now blogging. Monte and Amy write the monthly "Starstruck" astrology horoscope blog for Bergdorf Goodman's 5th/58th blog. Monte's remarkable insights and down-to-earth advice have been endorsed by leading visionary authors and company executives who use his unique skills as part of their important decision-making mix.

For further information, address:
Monte Farber
Post Office Box 2299
East Hampton, NY 11937
E-mail: info@TheEnchantedWorld.com
Web Site: www.TheEnchantedWorld.com

Follow Monte on Facebook
www.facebook.com/EnchantedWorld
and Twitter
www.twitter.com/#!/AskMonte

MONTE AND AMY'S POPULAR TITLES INCLUDE:

Karma Cards

The Enchanted Tarot

Instant Tarot Reader

Tarot Discovery Kit

True Love Tarot

Zerner/Farber Tarot Deck

Tarot Secrets

The Soulmate Path: Relationship Secrets

The Enchanted Birthday Book

Goddess, Guide Me!

The Enchanted Spellboard

Chakra Meditation Kit

The Psychic Circle Magical Message Board

The Pathfinder Psychic Talking Board

The GhostWriter Automatic Writing Kit

Little Reminders: Love & Relationships

Little Reminders: The Law of Attraction

The Truth Fairy Pendulum Kit

Astrology Gems: 12 Little Sun Sign Books

The Mystic Messenger

Wish Upon A Star

Secrets of The Fortune Bell

33 Ways to Tell Your Future

Healing Crystals

Acknowledgments

Life would be meaningless without those we care about, the living and those living in one or more of quantum physics' alternate universes. I could not have created *Quantum Affirmations* without the loving support of the following wonderful beings.

Amy Zerner

Rune Lind

Kristine Pidkameny

Jan Johnson

Michael Kerber

Michele Harper

Meg Floss

Colette Gilbert

David Rattiner

Kirsten Louise Lewis

Kate Mueth

Fred Soroka

Calixte Stamp

John Okas

Ellen Jo Myers

Cynthia Battaglia

Joyce Brian

Dan Romer

Rose Sheifer-Wright

Eileen Chetti

Jessie Spicer Zerner

Mr. Zane